WHO AM I?

I Am Who I Am Says I Am: Discovering Yourself In The Midst Of A Crisis

Nahchon D. Guyton

Who Am I. Copyright © 2020. Nahchon D. Guyton. All rights reserved.

No part of this book may be reproduced, stored in a retrieval system, or transmitted in any form or by any means, electronic, mechanical, photocopying, recording or otherwise, without prior permission of the author.

Published by:

ISBN: 978-1-949343-79-3 (paperback)

ISBN: 978-1-949343-80-9 (eBook)

Scripture taken from the New King James Version®. Copyright © 1982 by Thomas Nelson. Used by permission. All rights reserved.

For more information on Nahchon D. Guyton, visit www.nahchon.com and feel free to leave your comments and opinions about this book and your personal journey.

DEDICATION

I dedicate this book to my Heavenly Father, who loved me first.

To my eldest Brother in the kingdom, Jesus the Christ, who suffered death in my place that I may have a chance to choose life.

To my Comforter, Counselor and Friend, the Holy Spirit, who guides, directs and teaches me His ways, so I can continue to grow and be transformed into a Son of the most high God who rules the Kingdom of Heaven.

TABLE OF CONTENTS

Dedication iii
Preface 7
   What Is An Identity Crisis? 11
   Here Is The Guide To The Answers: 19
Introduction 23
Chapter 1: Life Is Filled With Stories 29
   The Early Years 31
   Lesson In The Story 34
Chapter 2: Johnathon's Mother 37
   Lesson In The Story 39
Chapter 3: JJ: The Key Whisper 41
   Lesson In The Story 46
Chapter 4: Ross "The Voice" Jones 49
   The Courtship 59
   The Accident 60
   Nurse Sarah 63
   Cindy's Conversion 66

A Child Is Born 71
Lesson In The Story 72
Chapter 5: The Search For Family 75
Enter Buck Jones A.K.A. Mr. B 76
Intermission In The Story 82
3-Jay Hears Voices 84
Tragedy Strikes, Yet Again 89
A New Hope Of Something Better 93
Out On The Town 99
The Youth Jam 106
3-Jay's Awakening 107
The Lesson 111
Chapter 6: I Am Who I AM Says I Am 115
God Created Us To Do What He Does 119
Chapter 7: False Reflections 125
Identity Is What Drives Us 130
Chapter 8: Who Told You That You Were Naked? ... 137
Chapter 9: Letter From Our Heavenly Father 145
Chapter 10: We Are Not Who We Think We Are. We Are More, Much More 151
Chapter 11: Stop Trying To Be What They Want And Start To Be What He Wants 161
I AM Says The Following 165
Here Is Who Jesus Said He Was 194

PREFACE

You may have heard the term "identity crisis" and you probably have a reasonably good idea what it implies. But where did this thought begin? Why do individuals experience this kind of personal crisis? Is it something limited to the young years? The concept begins within the work of formative psychologist Erik Erikson, who believed that the arrangement of personality was one of the foremost critical parts of a person's life. While creating a sense of character is an imperative portion of the adolescent years, Erikson did not accept that the arrangement and development of personality were just limited to youth. Instead, identity is something that shifts and develops all throughout life as individuals go up against modern challenges and handle distinctive encounters.

Today, everyone wants to self identify. Men want to be identified as women and girls want to be identified as boys; white people want to be identified as black, and black people want to be identified as white. When it comes to identity, it is more than a name, title or brand. It goes deeper than that. True identity is connected directly to your purpose. Who you are is more than what you call yourself.

What is identity at the basic level?

Whatever we call it, that is its name. When it comes to true identity, it goes beyond just calling it something. Identity is locked into our spiritual DNA. It is as unique to us as our finger prints.

Identity can be defined as who we are and what we do when no one else is looking. It is also how we are seen by the world. In a natural sense, identity is a part of our core character. It is wrapped up in our personality and knitted together by our purpose. Who we are is why we were created. A car is only a car because of its purpose, which is mobile transportation. A toaster is a toaster because it toasts things. Its purpose is its identity, not what we call it alone. I can stand in the garage, call myself a car and change my name to car, but no matter what I do, will I be able to function in all aspects as a car? I will be seen as a person and not a car. My function, purpose, and characteristics must align with my name in order for me to be identified as that thing. The purpose is never given by the product but by the creator. A car does not get to decide its purpose; only the manufacture can tell the car what it was created for. We are no different; we must go to the Creator to know why we are here.

The word "identity" is described in the Webster 1828 dictionary as: *noun Sameness, as distinguished from similitude and diversity.* We speak of the identity of goods found, the identity of persons, or of personal identity. What does sameness refer to? Its purpose, function, and characteristics must equal its name. This is what gives people, places and things identity.

Gender fluid, pansexual or gender-neutral sounds hip and tolerant, inclusive and accepting but, in reality, it is a lie from the pit of hell. If you are a male, born a male and have the parts of a male, you are a male. Even if you don't want to be male, no matter what you do, it will not change who you are and why you were created. The desire to be "other than" is not because that is who you are, but because you are hurting and you are in the middle of a crisis. You have lost sight of the big picture and have focused in on this minute moment in time. You are making permanent decisions based on fleeting circumstances. That is a crisis, that is pain, discomfort, confusion or, worse, rebellion.

We are in the middle of an identity crisis, lost in the political correctness of the moment. We think we get to choose our true identity. We were created for a purpose by a Creator and only the Maker gets to choose our identity. We don't get to choose that. Our identity is tied to our purpose and our purpose is linked to our mission for living. We are here because we have a purpose. If there is no purpose, there is no reason to be. Stop looking for an escape clause from your life. You are more than what happened to you, you are more than what someone said to you or about you. I know it hurts and the pain is real, and all you want is relief from this deep, soul-crushing pain that you are in. This is a crisis. It is not the end but a start to know and discover your true identity.

You mean more to the world than someone who has been raped, sexually assaulted and emotionally, physically and verbally abused. It was wrong and it should not have happened to you, and God was not in it, but He was with you going through it and working it all out for your good. Sadly, good things happen to bad people and bad things happen to good people. This is not uncommon in this life. Life is not fair, but it doesn't mean you don't matter. If God wanted you to be something other than how you were born, He would have made you that way. Embrace the you that you are, so you can become the you that God created you for.

What Is An Identity Crisis?

According to Erikson, a personality crisis could be a time of serious investigation into diverse ways of looking at oneself. Erikson claims his interest in character started in childhood. He often pondered the social life among the Yurok of Northern California and the Sioux of South Dakota, which made a difference in formalizing Erikson's thoughts about character advancement and character crisis. Erikson depicted the character as "a subjective sense as well as a perceptible quality of individual sameness and coherence, combined with a few convictions within the similarity and progression of a few shared world picture." Concurring to Marcia and his colleagues, the adjust between character and disarray lies in committing to an identity. Marcia, moreover, created a meet strategy to degree personality as well as four distinctive character statuses. This strategy looks at three distinctive regions of working: word related part, convictions and values, and sexuality. Identity accomplishment happens when a person has gone through an exploration.

Identity dissemination happens when there is no personality emergency or commitment. Those with a status of personality dissemination tend to feel out of place within the world and do not seek after a sense of character.

You have undoubtedly heard the term "identity crisis," but you may not know its origins. Identity achievement vs. identity diffusion is the fifth crisis that individuals experience as they navigate the potentially stormy years of adolescence. Perhaps for the first time in life, they contemplate their roles in society, including their careers, values, and gender role.

There are advantages to exploring your identity during your teenage years. This is the psychological state that Erikson called "identity achievement." If you do not come to grips with these crucial life decisions and never arrive at a firm identity, your "identity diffusion" will not prepare you for the developmental tasks that lie ahead.

A strong identity emerges from this conscious contemplation of your life's purpose and also from successfully resolving the developmental challenges that characterize the previous childhood years. Having a strong identity in adolescence rests, in part, on you having a strong sense of trust in infancy, autonomy in toddlerhood, ability to play as a preschooler, and solid work ethic in the elementary school years. Young people coping with the death of someone close to them, or even their own terminal illness, may face psychosocial issues associated with issues later in adulthood.

Let us get back to the question of identity. An "identity crisis" may occur at any time in your adult years when you are faced with a challenge to your sense of self. In addition, some adolescents may not go through an identity crisis at all but instead accept the roles and values handed down by parents. Other adolescents remain in a permanent state of crisis.

Because there are more than two ways people navigate their adolescent identity issues, researchers following Erikson's theory expanded his concept of the identity crisis. Simon Fraser University psychologist, James Marcia, working at the University of Buffalo at the time, developed a framework that went on to stimulate a large body of work on adolescent identity development. Called "identity statuses," Marcia defined four alternate ways that teenagers resolve identity issues.

The four identity statuses are built from high and low positions on two identity dimensions. People high on commitment have a firm sense of who they are and feel strongly about the choices they have made. People low in identity commitment have an uncertain sense of self. If you are high on the exploration dimension, you are actively questioning your sense of self and looking for ways to come to a decision.

Combining the high and low points on each dimension, we arrive at four identity statuses.

- People high on the commitment and exploration dimension are the traditional "identity achieved."

- At the opposite pole, on both dimensions, people low in commitment and exploration fit Erikson's criteria for "identity diffused."

- People high on exploration but low on commitment are in a category that Marcia called "moratorium."
- The final category applies to people who are low on exploration and high on commitment.

The most favorable status for people to have in terms of adjustment is identity achieved. People who are in the moratorium category, at least during adolescence, will be the most likely to fit the classic image of the rebellious teen. The identity diffuse can also experience difficulties because they tend to float and may be led astray and into high-risk behaviors. The problem for them is that without an actual period of exploring their own commitments, they may find themselves in mid-life regretting those decisions that did not match their true, inner needs.

The identity statuses were originally meant to apply to adolescents, but later researchers have extended them to the adult years. In looking at adults, though, the natural question to ask is whether an identity exploration in adolescence is enough to keep people optimally adapted in adulthood. Several identity researchers, including me, examined the commitment and exploration dimensions as continuous developmental processes that can carry on throughout life. Just because you experienced a period of identity exploration as a teen doesn't mean you are set for life. It is healthy to keep exploring your values, roles, and sense of self, regardless of your age.

There are various questionnaires that identity researchers use to measure identity statuses or the dimensions that produce them. The quiz gives you a quick assessment of which identity status is closest to how you are right now.

The questions cover four identity commitments: politics, religion, career choices, and gender roles, which are the areas covered by the identity status measures used in the literature.

For each question, pick the choice that is closest to the way you feel right now:

1. Politics is something:

   a) I can never be too sure about because things change so fast. But I do think it is important to know what I can politically stand for and believe in.

   b) I haven't really considered because it doesn't excite me much.

   c) I feel pretty much the same way about as my family. I follow what they do in terms of voting and such.

   d) I have thought it through. I realize I can agree with some and not other aspects of what my family believes.

2. When it comes to religion:

   a) I am not sure what religion means to me. I would like to make up my mind, but I am not done looking yet.

   b) I don't give religion much thought and it doesn't bother me one way or the other.

   c) I have gone through a period of serious questions about faith and can now say I understand what I believe in as an individual.

   d) I have never really questioned my religion. If it is right for my family, it must be right for me.

3. Regarding my career choice:

   a) I haven't really settled on a career. I am just taking whatever jobs are available until something good comes along.

   b) I am still trying to decide where my career interests lie and actively thinking about what jobs will be right for me.

c) I thought a little about my career, but there is never really any question since my parents decided what they want for me.

d) It took me a while to figure it out, but now I really know I am on the right career path.

4. With regard to men's and women's roles:

a) My views are identical to those of my family. What has worked for them will obviously work for me.

b) I have never really seriously considered men's and women's roles. It just doesn't seem to concern me.

c) I have spent some time thinking about men's and women's roles and I have decided what works best for me.

d) There are so many ways to define men's and women's role; I am trying to decide what will work for me.

Here Is The Guide To The Answers:

Politics:

a – Moratorium | b – Diffuse | c – Foreclosed | d - Achieved

Religion:

a – Moratorium | b – Diffuse | c – Achieved | d - Foreclosed

Career:

a – Diffuse | b - Moratorium | c – Foreclosed | d - Achieved

Gender Role:

a - Foreclosed | b – Diffuse | c – Achieved | d - Moratorium

While adding up your totals, you may have a mix of the four identity statuses, but it is likely that you will lean more towards one than another. People in the moratorium status, as long as they don't stay there forever, simply need more time or perhaps the chance to continue their exploration before they are forced to make a choice. The problem with the diffuse status is that the longer you float on these important areas, the less likely it is you will shore up your sense of self enough to handle your future developmental challenges. For example, it is difficult to establish true intimacy, if your identity is weak.

In the areas for which you are rated foreclosed, you can benefit from taking a step back and engaging in some serious exploration. In contrast to these three negatively oriented trajectories, people who continually evaluate their commitments and make adjustments to achieve greater realization of their identities ("authentic road") are most likely to achieve fulfillment throughout their lives.

This quiz, though brief, can give you a quick snapshot of where you stand on a developmental task that maintains its centrality in your personality and ability to adapt to your life's challenges. You can also use this tool to help advise your own teenagers, students, advisees, and clients to provide them with a sense of where they may need to move up or down the exploration or commitment scales.

Keep your mind open, but not too open, toward change. Your identity can adapt to whatever developmental tasks come your way.[1]

How can you tell if you are having an identity emergency? Whereas we all question who we are from time to time, you are having an identity emergency if you are going through an enormous alter or unpleasant time in life and the following questions begin to meddle along with your way of life:

- Who am I? This question may be in general or in regards to your relationships, age, and/or career.

- What are my values?

- What is my role in society or purpose in life?

- What are my spiritual beliefs?

- What am I passionate about?

In physcology, they often try to sterilize these questions by making them something scientific, when in

---

[1] *Excerpt from Susan Krauss Whitbourne, Ph.D. 2012*

reality it goes much deeper. It is a matter of soul and spirit. Yes, this is true as to what can cause a character emergency i.e. identity crisis, but it does not answer the questions: *Who am I? Why am I here? What is my true purpose?* Remember this is what the product thinks about why it was made. You are a product of the Creator, and He has a grand plan for why He created you. He is the only one who can answer these questions fully. Everyone else is just guessing.

It is my goal to give you a spirit-led perspective on these questions with some practical ways of dealing with this crisis that most people go through at some point in their lives.

INTRODUCTION

This is a deeper dive into where I concluded my last book "One Journey 7 Ships." It was something I felt pressed to write about in order to provoke questions and get people to think about who they really are. This book is a deep dive into the subject of "Who am I really?" We all have something to give, but most of us will not share it because we do not know who we are or what our purpose is. We don't value what we carry enough to share it with the world.

This book is not going to be a typical book telling you who you are. Instead, this book will prepare you to accept, question and reason through why you have not been what you were created to be. It is my hope that the pages of this book will help you unlock yourself from within yourself so you begin to walk in the light that you came to the planet to share with the world.

Open your mind and heart, and prepare to meet the greatest gift this world has ever seen; the true you.

> *"Confront the dark parts of yourself, and work to banish them with illumination and forgiveness. Your willingness to wrestle with your demons will cause your angels to sing."*
>
> ~ August Wilson

Is life about experiences, stories, and events, or is it perhaps about something else?

> *"Wanting to be someone else is a waste of the person you are."*
>
> ~ Marilyn Monroe

We all ask these questions at some point in our lives:

1. Why am I here?
2. What can I do?
3. Do I have anything of value to offer?
4. Am I of any value?
5. What is my value/purpose?
6. Who am I, really?
7. Why was I born?
8. What can I do well?
9. Who wants me, the real me?

10. Am I even necessary?

These questions, and many more like them, shape us into feeling like we don't matter. What we believe is what we live and that becomes the life we live. Our current life may not have been the designed for us, but because we believe that it is who we are, we live life accordingly. We are a cosmic mosaic of all our experiences, hurt, pain and triumphs. They shape our perspective of the world; they aid us in our growth, but they don't make our life; our faith and fears do that. Our fears tell us that we are less than and can shape us into a dark, brooding person who plays it safe when it comes to sharing our true selves with others. In essence, we become prisoners of our fears. Our faith, on the other hand, tells us that we will get past this too; we can do it, and no matter the challenge, we can overcome it. We become confident, adventurous lovers of people and experiences. We live life to the fullest without limits and unashamed of failure. Failure to all who live and walk by faith is just another lesson to learn something new; it is never a reason to stop doing or being your best self. Failure is simply fuel for the next adventure, it does not stop us but propel us forward with focus, assurance, and tenacity.

Often we trust lies and rebuke truth with great vigor, fighting to uphold the lies as we deliberately search for anything we can find to uphold the lies we tell ourselves. "What is truth?" is the question on most of your minds. Some lies you tell yourself are, for example, you are *no one special, you are insignificant or, the worse lie of all, you do not matter.* So what is the truth? The truth is, **you are extremely valuable.** The fact that you are here means you have great worth and much to contribute. You came to the planet with a unique set of skills, which only you can do. Truth is, your true value will not be known until you accept the fact that you need others to help you be your best self. You will never reach the pinnacle of who you are created to be until you believe in yourself and act accordingly. You are a deep treasure filled with vast wealth, mixed with trash and toxic waste. Treasure hunting is not for the faint of heart; it takes work.

As we uncover some treasures and secrets that have been hiding in plain sight, we will be able to answer the question, "Who am I?" We will also debunk age-old lies and reveal the traps that we all fall into, that is, identity crisis and the feeling that we are worthless.

Lastly, I want to introduce you to a precious, treasure-packed gift that has not been opened. This gift has laid dormant, un-sparked, unmotivated for as long as you have had breath. That gift that was the purpose for your creation, design, and manufacturing of you. You carry a gift, and you were created with a purpose of sharing that gift. The gift you carry is for the world, but only you can give it. You may have heard this all your life or you may have never heard these words spoken to you, about you or over you. Prior to going any further, let me say this to you:

> You are special; a unique person with something that the world needs. You are an answer to a prayer, a solution to a problem and inspiration to a hopeless situation. You are valuable; your value far exceeds the Dow Jones, NASDAQ and S&P. Your worth is without measure. You are one in a trillion to trillion power. Yet, with all of that, you are living beneath your purpose and walking in defeat instead of victory, questioning your very existence.

STOP IT, RIGHT NOW! *Make a bold choice to be who you were created to be.*

Walking the Earth with a weighted heart wandering, confused and, often, angered by this question you ask yourself in secret, afraid to answer aloud because someone may hear. You whisper to yourself deep, deep within yourself: "Who am I?" Let us unpack that question and discover the answers together. Let us start with a story.

Chapter 1
LIFE IS FILLED WITH STORIES

Stories, as we are taught in journalism school early on, are told through people. Those stories make our documentaries powerful. You can explore someone's culture, you can explore their experience,

Who Am I?

> *you can explore an issue through human beings who are going through it.*
>
> *~ Soledad O'Brien*

Johnathon was seventeen and homeless. He went from shelter to shelter trying to find a place to lay his music-filled head. He was a pleasant kid, despite all the tragedy he had endured. Some, or maybe even most, questioned what was going on with this kid that hurt, pain and suffering loomed over him like a dark storm-laden cloud. Wherever he went, tragedy seemed to be close behind. Why love, laugh and be happy when, around the corner, the next catastrophic event is waiting to pounce on you as a hungry cat pounces on a mouse, they would say to themselves.

Johnathon had been homeless for the last two years. His mom, Cindy, died of a rare heart condition when he was ten. He went to live with his only known living relative, a great uncle by the name of Buck Jones. Everyone called him Mr. B, including Johnathan, who went by the nicknames 3-Jay, Jay3 or John Jay. Mr. B. died two years ago and 3-Jay became homeless and on the streets wandering and wondering how he was going to make it.

Before we can go forward, we must look back, not to relive the past but to unearth the lessons of the past. We are going to go back in time to discover how Johnathon ended up being homeless and what jewels we can unpack as we go through his story.

The Early Years

Johnathon was named Johnathon Jason Jones, which is kind of a mouth full, plus there were three Johnathons in his kindergarten class, so his friends started calling him 3-Jay. Johnathon was born in Memphis, Tennessee. Soon after he was born, his mother went back to a Houston Suburb, where she and Johnathon's father were living before he died. He was one of only four black kids in his class. He often felt alone because the other three were girls and they were all mixed with something else. The story goes that since he was the last and third Johnathon to enter the class, he became 3-Jay or Jay-3.

3-Jay stuck to Johnathon almost instantly, so everyone called him 3-Jay or Jay-3 when they got excited. He took to both names and just flowed with it. 3-Jay was a musical prodigy. He could play any instrument just from hearing someone play it only once. 3-Jay was a huge fan of the saxophone and the acoustic guitar; those were his favorites. He could play anything he heard. He could sing as well, but he rarely showed that side of his musical repertoire.

He did not like being called 3-Jay in the beginning but it sort of grew on him after some time. He was quiet, pleasant but lacked identity so he felt invisible. Johnathon was muscular, musical and had no real interest in sports. His appearance made most think he would be a great athlete and they treated him as such. This was far from the truth; he was just born with an athletic build, with the mind and heart of a philosopher, musician and scientist. 3-Jay was caring, charming and so articulate that the teachers often commented. Initially, 3-Jay hated his muscular build because he thought people would not take him seriously. He felt most people only saw his size and began to treat him like some dumb-jock.

Though he never met his father, when he relaxed and let his true self out, he was just like his father. 3-Jay seemed to lack the confidence and internal identity of his father, so he rarely relaxed and showed his true self. 3-Jay often felt abandoned and lonely. He was confused about who he was supposed to be. He never felt comfortable being his true self. His lack of comfort with who he was kept him in hiding. He was hiding in plain sight. He only shared small parts of himself, often hiding behind his size. He looked intimidating, so he used it to keep people away and from getting too close. 3-Jay longed for a true connection with people, but found it easier to hide behind his size. He was never really interested in sports, but felt drawn to it as a way of connecting with people. His mother was not going to let him play sports. She felt he had more to offer the world than just being an athlete. *"I am destined to be alone,"* He told himself, *"This is how it was going to be; I will always be alone in a room full of people."* No one really saw him for who he was. His thought was, *"I don't even know who I am. Mom won't let me play sports, and I am afraid to join the band. I don't know what to do, except go along with who they think I am."*

His mother was a famous Jazz vocalist who traveled often. She started out on the Black College Tour, going to small clubs along the southern border of the United States. She was determined to do what she enjoyed and loved and that was music. She was hitting various Jazz Clubs; big ones, small ones, and makeshift ones. 3-Jay's mother, Cindy, had done very well for herself financially because she poured herself into her music. She often told 3-Jay to do the same, but he just would not do it. He made every excuse as to why he could not let music be his companion, guide and friend. He wanted more, but was afraid to do what he was gifted to do. He wanted what he thought, and refused to accept what he already had: music.

Lesson In The Story

Sometimes we accept names and titles that we don't like, so we can be liked. Often we hide our true nature, gifts and talents from the world, so the dim lit world will not be blinded by our bright shining light. Do not turn down your light for the world. Instead, turn it up and let it shine bright. Sometimes we use our perceived self to protect our real self. 3-Jay looked intimidating so he used it to keep people away and from getting too close. In his effort to protect himself, he imprisoned himself. Even though he longed for a true connection with people, he carcerated himself, because he was afraid. Isolation and separation was his cloak; loneliness was his dagger. He kept what he wanted the most at bay. He found it easier to hide behind his size than to be himself. We are all like 3-Jay in this; we hide behind our masks and refuse to come out. Then we tell our self a lie and that lie is: *"No one cares. I am nobody. No one will miss me. I have no value or purpose."*

Truth is, you are a precious gem in the jewelry box of the world. You need to be seen for the gem you are.

No one will see you, if you continue to turn down your light. Let your light shine. Be you and everything else will fall into place. STOP working so hard to be someone else. Consider this: you are the only one who can do what you can. This is what makes you valuable. They, them or the others are just that; they could never be you, and you will never be them. Enjoy the you that you are and know that you are enough.

Chapter 2
3 JAY'S MOTHER

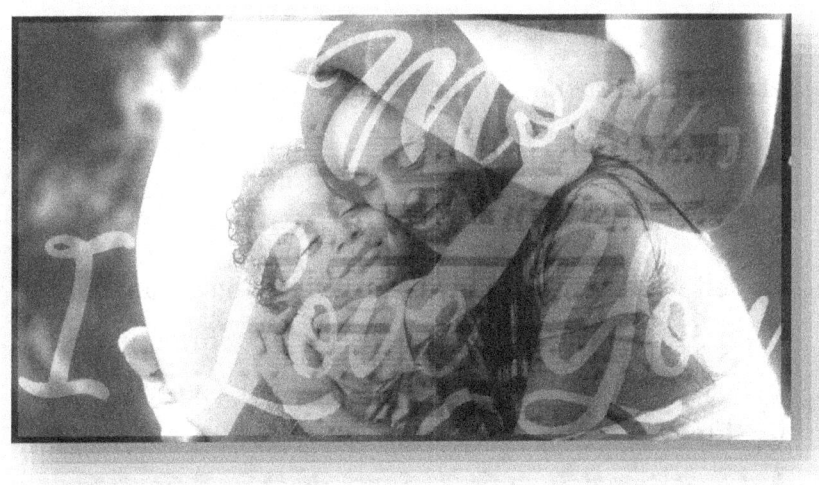

Cindy was sort of a free spirit; extremely beautiful and highly intelligent. When it came to romantic relationships, not so much. She thought relationships were a distraction, maybe because she was actually a little awkward when it came to matters of the heart. Cindy was in love with music. She often looked at intimate relationships as a hindrance, a bother, a distraction and something that could keep her from her first love: music.

She was beautiful, talented and could probably have any man she wanted, but she was focused on her craft, her gift, her treasure, which was her love: music. Cindy would often tell herself everything was either an obstacle or a step to get her closer or take her further away from her goals. Cindy said: *"If it's an obstacle, I am going to go around it, over it or through it, but nothing will keep me from my first love, music."*

Cindy's goal was simply to be the best vocalist and musician she could be. She was never one to compare herself to anyone. Others would compare her to the Lena Horns, Mahalia Jackson, Aretha Franklin, Etta James, Whitney Houston and Mariah Carey's of the world. When they did, Cindy would reply, *"Thank you, but I am just doing me. They did them, and I want to do me. No need to compare. I could never do them and they could never be me."*

Many men have tried to court and get Cindy's attention, but music was her love. No man could be more to her than music has been. She was once quoted in a Jazz publication:

"Music is my first love. It held me when no one else could or would; it carried me when I was down and it stood by me when I wanted to give up. Music is my heartbeat, my pulse, my lover and friend. It's my beginnings, my middle and will be my end."

Cindy met a piano player on one of her road trips. They called him JJ, the Ivory Keys Whisperer. He could play some of the best jazz piano you ever heard. He was great on the keys and terrible when it came to being a mature man. He acted like a child once he got off the stage, almost as if he had some type of learning disability. JJ was smart, genuine, playful and forever young at heart. Most people often thought he must have autism or something. JJ and Cindy became best friends, like sister and brother. JJ would eventually introduce Cindy to his best friend from High School, Ross Jones.

Lesson In The Story

Cindy knew who she was and embraced it fully. She was determined to be her best. She was in love and music was his name. Cindy was determined to do her and to be her best. We all should strive for that very same thing. Don't let life get in the way of you pouring yourself out and developing your gift to its full capacity. We are originals; no need to compare us to other originals. No matter how hard it gets, if you stick with your love, like Cindy, you will be rewarded at the proper time.

> "Others would compare her to the Lena Horns, Mahalia Jackson, Aretha Franklin, Etta James, Whitney Houston and Mariah Carey's of the world. When they did, Cindy would reply, *'Thank you, but I am just doing me. They did them, and I want to do me. No need to compare.'*"

Chapter 3
JJ: THE KEY WHISPERER

JJ was a great jazz piano player; he was a kid at heart: fun, loving, tender and genuine. He was in a state of extended adolescence. He cared more about being free to do what he wanted, that he refused to grow up and become fully responsible. When JJ was in school, he was awkward, social but not well acquainted with the social norms. He would often say and do what most would call inappropriate. He was good-natured, smart and loved people. He grew up in the Midwest and he never knew is father or mother. They died when he was very young, so he lived with his uncle and aunt (sister of his mother). His uncle was a building engineer/designer and his aunt was a bank manager. They both loved music, so every night they would come home, put on some music and dance. JJ was musical, but didn't know it. It was hidden until he was exposed to the key or keys that would unlock his treasure chest.

When JJ was about two years old, his uncle brought home an old piano he got from a building he was scheduled to redesign. JJ sat down at the piano and started playing the song that was on the stereo. It was "Misty Blue" by Dorothy Moore. He played it perfectly, and once the song ended, he continued to play. His aunt and uncle were amazed. They thought it was a fluke, so the uncle wanted to test him. He put on some Ray Charles to see, and yes, JJ played it perfectly, except for one of the notes. The uncle said, "Hey, JJ, try this." He put on some Cedar Walton Quartet "Fantasy in D." JJ listened, smiled and began to play. "This kid has some talent," Uncle said, "We have to invest in him. We have to put him in classes or something."

JJ never got to take those classes until he was in Middle School where he first met Ross Jones. Ross was starting his own band, and needed someone to play the piano. JJ said, "I can play for you."

Ross moved away for a year. They reconnected in High School. JJ was still socially awkward, not knowing what he should and should not say in certain situations. JJ believed in telling the truth, regardless. He had no filter. If he thought something was ugly, he would say it. If he felt you were being rude, he would tell you. It didn't matter who you were, if he had something to say, you could count on JJ to let it be known.

One day, JJ was in the lunch room talking to some girls and one of their boyfriends walked over and asked, "Why are you talking to my girl?" JJ, without hesitation, said, "Because she is nice and I wanted to talk to her." Most people would have left it there, but not JJ. He said, "Besides, you weren't talking to her anyway." This did not go over too well. The guy started to push on JJ, and in walked Ross. JJ was not a push-over by any stretch of the imagination. He did not like to use violence, unless he had to. He preferred to fight with words and honesty.

Ross walked up and said, "Hey, is there a problem here?" Ross was 6 feet 2 inches, 220 pounds, and naturally muscular. JJ said, "Hey, RJ, what's up? When did you get back into town?" Ross looked at the girl's boyfriend and asked again, "Is there an issue?" The guy looked at Ross and responded, "No. We were just leaving." The guy walked away. JJ turned to Ross and said, "You know, I could handle myself."

Ross said, "I know that, but I don't need you being suspended for beating up a kid and then talking bad about him as well." They laughed and continued talking to the girls.

JJ was always playing the piano, every chance he got. He went to the bandroom and played before and after school. One day, while he was playing, the new school choir director walked in and started to yell at him for being in there, but he did not hear her. Then she paused and just listened to him play. He did not notice her there, until she said something. JJ smiled and said, "I am sorry, I didn't know anyone was here."

She said, "Young man, you play very well. Who taught you?"

JJ heard that question a lot; most people did not beleive the truth that he had it in him from birth. He would just start naming famous jazz piano players and that would end the inquisition almost immediately. JJ said, "To be honest, no one. I have been playing the piano since I was 2 or 3."

"Really," she replied, "I noticed that you had some hard key changes that could be a little smoother."

He said, "Where? I nailed that song."

She said, "You did, but when you made the cord change, it was a little harsh. Let me show you what I mean."

JJ said, "Sure."

She said, "Play the last part of the song."

He played and she played it along with him. When he went to make the cord change, she tapped his hand and placed his fingers on the keys to make the cord change without it sounding so harsh. She said, "Most wouldn't notice it, but I can hear it." He did what she instructed. It felt better than what he was doing before.

"Are you a part of the choir or the band?" She asked.

JJ replied, "I play with the jazz band here, but not a part of the choir."

She said, "I will make a deal with you. If you join the choir as our piano player, I will coach you with some of those cord changes."

JJ agreed. That was the first lesson he had in all his years of playing piano. JJ joined the choir and that was where he and Ross became best friends. All throughout high school, JJ and Ross were best friends working on music and playing in the band Ross formed. JJ kept playing for the choir up until he graduated. The Choir Director taught him how to make smooth transitions and how to push his gift even further. One of those pushes was when she told him she wanted him to play the piano like a drum and let it be the heartbeat of the song. That was when JJ realized that he could make those keys do whatever he set his mind to. She always said, "JJ, when you play. have fun. If it's not fun, you are not playing." He took those words to heart because he never seemed to stop playing on or off the stage. He just wanted it to be fun or he would not do it. Some musicians took this the wrong way and often got upset with JJ in rehearsal. JJ would practice as much as he could but he always wanted it to be fun, so he would play jokes on people, make weird sounds with the piano or just say something outlandish to break the seriousness of any moment. People would often say, "JJ can play, but sometimes, I think he plays too much." Ross never felt like that. He knew JJ was just trying to lighten the mood, so they clicked.

Lesson In The Story

JJ was a natural, but to get better, even naturals need coaching. We were not designed to do life alone. We can only go so far by ourselves; we need others to help sharpen us. We can go far, but we will never reach our full potential alone. Life is a team sport, and it requires all of us to connect with others to become our best.

In life, we often meet people and we don't know the impact they are going to have in our lives until we look back. The past is gone and can never be changed, but we can use it to shed some light on our current situation. Look back, but don't stay there. Some people will not understand you and that is fine; you just make sure you understand you. Don't change to fit in, be your best and those who are supposed to be with you will remain and show up right on time to give you the next piece of the puzzle. Be like JJ in this way: have fun living life, but know that even though stuff happens, don't let it change you for the worst but the better.

JJ played all the time. He, like Cindy, cultivated his gifts, harnessed it and let it carry him to the next level. What do you have that you have neglected? What is in your treasure chest that you keep hidden like 3-Jay? What is your first love? Are you being your authentic self, or are you so afraid of standing out that you often stand down when you should be standing up? Only you can answer all of these questions. Think about it and be honest with yourself when the answer comes.

Last question, have you been pretending to be dim, when in actuality you are a bright star? If your answer is yes, why? Let your light shine so the whole world can bask in the light that God put in you for them to enjoy. Don't ever dim yourself to let someone else feel comfortable. This does not mean you flaunt it; this means you own it.

Chapter 4
ROSS "THE VOICE" JONES

Ross "The Voice" Jones was a charmer, nice on the eyes, deep baritone voice with music in his tongue; this man could sing. When he starts singing, women would seem to lose their minds. Ross opened his mouth and let the song just float out. Women would faint, some have been know to cry. I am telling you, this man was gifted when it came to singing. His voice was deep, strong, light and clear.

He had "it": talent, gifting and a crazy effect on the ladies. Despite this effect on women, Ross was a perfect gentleman. He would often say: "I will never understand why women react that way." Ross was no fool; he used it to book more gigs. He actually came to expect it, so in the rare cases when he sang and women did not respond as they have in the past, he felt like he was off. He would say: "I have to step it up next set. Am I getting too comfortable? I have to be better next time."

When Ross saw Cindy, he was hooked. *She was so beautiful*, he thought to himself. When she started singing, it was a knock-out blow. Ross was down for the count. She had him at the first note. He couldn't think of another woman. He made up his mind to get to know this woman.

Cindy came in to do an impromptu rehearsal one day for a show she was doing that night. Ross was in the back of the Jazz Club where they were installing some new speakers and monitors for the show. Ross found himself in awe, then he understood a little bit more about the effect he had on women. He heard Cindy's voice and was at a loss, falling fast in love. Ross was frozen with delight, mouth open and eyes fixed on

Cindy. He could not move for a moment or two; he was in a trance of sorts. He knew at that moment that he had to make her his wife. He did not want to sleep with her; he wanted to marry her. In that brief moment, he saw a life with her. He visualized what it would be like to be married and have a family with her. Cindy had taken Ross's breath away and she had no clue. He was down for the count.

Only one problem: he did not know how to do it. He was so used to women coming to him, that he forgot how to approach them without being awkward and clumsy in his speech. He was so used to women falling all over themselves that he rarely had to say anything to them before they rushed him. He would often have to make up a story to get away from all of them. Some of his bandmates thought he was afraid of women. He would respond, "I respect them, even if they won't respect themselves."

JJ was friends with both Ross and Cindy. He made it his secret mission to get Cindy in a loving relationship. JJ felt Cindy was too beautiful, too caring and too great a person to be alone, but she was just not interested in guys like that. She liked them, but not more than her music. Most men became extremely jealous and overbearing with her when it came to her touring, doing shows and singing. No one could ever mistake Cindy for being average; she was stunning with a voice and spirit to match. Cindy never thought much about how she looked. She was in love with the music. She felt music was less complicated than relationships. She just wanted to sing and bring joy to people with her voice and musical gifts. Cindy was herself a savant; she could arrange, write and play anything from classical, to the latest hits on the radio.

Her passion was Jazz. She loved the emotions and freedom of Jazz. The heart of Jazz was to feel the music and go where it takes you. Cindy would often say she was married to her music and Jazz was her husband; he understood her and she understood him. "We move in rhythm, walk in melody and live in harmony," she would say, "Jazz is the perfect husband. His passion to move me is matched by my passion to move people. That's what I call a perfect union." This was always her response whenever someone inquired about why she was not married, being so breathtakingly beautiful and a voice that would make the angels in heaven take notice.

JJ saw Ross locked on Cindy and thought to himself, "They would make a great couple." Ross was known as RJ to his friends. RJ was always a perfect gentleman and he would have no problem with Cindy touring or doing what she loved, which was the same thing he loved; blessing people with good quality music. JJ said, "I am going to make this happen, after I have a little fun with RJ." JJ called to RJ, "RJ, RJ, close your mouth, and take a picture, it would last longer. RJ, RJ come on, man, we have to finish this before the show. RJ, still in awe?" JJ walked up to him and tapped him on the shoulder. "RJ, RJ, what's the matter with you man?"

"Nothing, she is amazing."

"Who?" JJ tried to play it off.

RJ said, "Cindy."

"Oh yeah, and man can she sing."

RJ lightly punches JJ on the arm. JJ asked, "What was that for?"

"I heard what you said about closing my mouth and all." They both laughed and started to walk towards the back.

JJ finally asked, "Do you want me to introduce you two?"

RJ responded, "Yeah, right. Like you know her, know her."

JJ said, "No, for real, Cin and I like brother and sister. Do you want me to make the introduction or does Ross 'the Voice' Jones got this?"

Ross said, with excitement, "Make the introduction. JJ, don't be messing around with me. You do know her, right?"

"Yeah, man. I know her. We go way back, like High top fades and Cadillacs." They both burst out laughing.

RJ said, "Man, you are crazy."

They start walking to the back where they were working. RJ said, "I thought you were going to make the introduction."

"I will, but we have to get these screens hung for the show."

"Come on, JJ, stop playing and make the introduction."

"Man, you must really be feeling this one. You usually run away and act like you don't know what to do."

"Whatever, man. Make the introduction." They turned and walked towards the stage.

"Cin, Cindy, Cindy," JJ called. She took out her earpiece and turned to see JJ. She ran and gave him a big hug.

"Hey, J, what's going on. I didn't know you were here yet, being a big-time club owner and all."

"I don't know about big time, but I wanted to hang some screens and extra speakers before the show tonight. Thank you again for doing this show for me, you really came through for me."

Cindy smiled and said, "You know you my brother from another mother." They continued to laugh and catch up.

RJ was getting anxious. He bumped JJ with his shoulder. JJ said, "Let me introduce you to someone very special to me. He is my brother from another mother. Cin, this is Ross Jones."

RJ interrupts, "My friends call me RJ."

Cindy was never one to let anyone know what she was really thinking. She said, "Mr. Jones, so we are friends now?"

"No, but, I mean, I, we could…" He couldn't seem to get the words out. Cindy saw him struggle, smiled a little and extended her hand.

"Nice to meet you, Ross."

"You can call me RJ."

"We are not friends yet, so, for now, I will call you Ross."

Cindy was feeling RJ, she just did not know how to take it or him. She had never felt that way about anybody, especially on the first meeting. Cindy thought to herself, "Girl, you trippin', you don't know him. He could be some crazy guy. Who knows, but man is he cute. I am gonna stop thinking about this and get back to my first love, this music." Cindy went on with her rehearsal, but her mind kept falling back on RJ.

A few months passed and she was back in town. She stopped in to see JJ one night. RJ was there and he asked her out to dinner. Cindy played it off. The only reason she came to the club was to see if RJ was there. RJ was performing that night. Cindy had never seen or heard him sing. She thought he was like all the other performers; good but nothing remarkable. Oh, how mistaken she was. RJ said, "I have to go on now. Give me your answer when I finish this set."

"Sure, RJ, I will have an answer for you when you're done. Don't be surprised if it's no," She smiled.

"RJ," he said, "You called me RJ? I guess we are friends now." He walked on to the stage and did his thing. Just like clockwork, all the women were mesmerized. Cindy was right along with them, caught up in the moment. JJ walked over and said, "Hey Cin, what got your mouth all open?"

JJ knew what was going on; he just liked messing with folks.

"You know I don't care for you calling me Cin. It just sounds bad."

"Cin ain't never sounded or looked so good."

"You never saw Ross 'the Voice' Jones do his thing?" JJ asked.

Cindy said, "He is amazing. His voice is so smooth, and he has so much control. It's almost like he is playing the piano with his voice."

"Oh, yeah. My boy is bad," JJ said.

"He has these women in here about to lose their minds. I mean, they be going crazy for your boy."

"Every night he makes up an excuse why he can't go home with them."

"He does?" Cindy asked, "What does he usually say?"

"He tells them he is married and his wife would not approve."

"Is he married?" Cindy asked, alarmed.

"No, only to his music."

Cindy smiled, "Really?"

"Yeah, he is quite serious about his music and you," JJ slipped the last part in quietly.

"What did you say?"

"What did you hear?"

"Nothing. I thought you said something."

JJ knew she heard him but he didn't want to be too obvious.

"I'll see you in a bit. I have to make my rounds." JJ said.

"Bye. See ya."

Cindy sat there enjoying the show and anxiously waiting for RJ to end his set. RJ did his last song and began to walk off the stage. Women started crowding around the stage as they normally do. RJ, never rude, said, "Ladies, ladies, have some respect. That is my wife over there," he was pointing at Cindy. The women quickly dispersed, except for one woman. She was determined to get RJ. Cindy saw him in a situation and walked up and said, "Are you ready?" The woman turned and left.

"Thank you. These women can be a trip." RJ said. Without missing a step, "So, what is your answer?"

"My answer? My answer to what?" Cindy was flirting.

"About me taking you out for dinner."

"Let me see, I think I will let you take me out for dinner."

"Yes," RJ celebrated.

"You seem a little excited about dinner. You must like to eat or something."

"No, I am excited about you."

"Oh, Really?"

"Yes."

The Courtship

They started dating off and on for a few years. They never actually broke up, they just did not spend a lot of time together with Ross touring and Cindy doing the same. There were periods of 6-8 months where they did not see each other. They spoke on the phone when schedules allowed, but both remained true to the long distance-short distance kind of relationship. Cindy was okay with it. She had someone to talk to who understood music, touring and her love of music. Ross wanted more, he wanted to make Cindy his wife, and he wanted to start a family with her.

He proposed twice, but Cindy declined on both occasions. Cindy was afraid of letting someone fall in love with her because she did not know if her next breath was her last. No one knew she had a rare medical condition, not even JJ, and she told him just about everything. He was like her brother and they were really close.

Cindy had a twin fraternal brother, not identical. Her brother, Charles, died while he was swimming at youth camp when he was just nine years old. Charles suffered from a rare heart disease that would eventually take Cindy's life. Since that dreadful day, she vowed never to get too close to anyone, in a romantic way at least. She was thinking about that promise she made herself when RJ asked her to marry him.

RJ was a charmer, so on the third time, Cindy gave in, almost five years to the day from when he first asked. They got married some years later. They were happy and loving music and each other and she became pregnant.

The Accident

RJ did not know Cindy was pregnant and he was going to be a dad. When Cindy found out, she called RJ and told him she wanted to discuss their immediate future together. RJ thought nothing of it because Cindy always spoke in the here and now. He thought maybe she wanted to travel to some exotic place and teach music to the natives. Cindy was just that way; always willing to share music and her gifts with the world.

On his way home, RJ decided to stop by the local ice cream shop and pick up some ice cream: strawberry mint cheesecake, which was Cindy's favorite. On his way back to the car, RJ was struck dead by a hit and run driver. No one saw anything; it happened suddenly, as if the vehicle just appeared out of nowhere. The vehicle struck RJ and ran over him and, just like that, RJ was gone without ever knowing he was going to be a father: one of his greatest wishes. He always wanted to be a father but he would never know the joys of fatherhood.

Cindy was preparing for RJ to come home. She was happy, worried, sad and deeply afraid all at the same time. She did not know what to expect, think or feel, or how she could raise a child. Since RJ was going to be a father, she was going to tell him more about her rare heart condition. In the past, she just played it down, never telling him how she could drop dead without warning at any moment. Cindy was often haunted by this. Knowing that her life was so uncertain, it created a deep well of fear in her that she could never let herself feel secure in being a mother, or a wife. She knew how much RJ wanted to be a father, so she stopped taking her birth control pills and let nature take its course.

Just as Cindy was getting lost in her well of fear and worry, she looked up and noticed that it was after eight and RJ did not show up. It was so unlike RJ; he was always home no later than 7:00. Cindy began to worry; she grabbed her cell phone and called his number, no answer. She called again, but still no answer. She called JJ and no answer. Now she was in a full-tilt worry mode spiraling fast toward despair. She had this gut-wrenching pain in her stomach telling her that RJ was gone; the same feeling she had when Charles, her twin brother, had passed.

Cindy tried to compose herself. She picked up the phone and prepared to dial RJ but at that moment her phone rang. The woman on the other side of the phone introduced herself as Sarah at the Emergency Room at the Local Medical Center. Cindy asked, "What happened? Is my husband okay." Cindy was beginning to get excited and not in a good way. She was breathing hard and not able to catch her breath.

Sarah said, "Ma'am, could you please take a breath. I need you to come down here now."

"Come down there for what? Is my husband okay? What is going on?"

"Could you please come down here? There has been an accident." Sarah did not want to tell the tragic news over the phone, "Please get down here as soon as possible?"

Cindy finally gained her composure and replied, "Yes, I will be there in 15 to 20 minutes."

Sarah said, "Okay. When you come to the hospital, go straight to the emergency room. Ask for me, Sarah Williams. I am the head nurse here at the hospital."

Cindy arrived at the hospital and she was filled with this inner knowing that it was not going to be good news. She asked for Sarah at the desk as instructed. Sarah came out, led her to a private waiting room and began to tell her that her husband was dead. Cindy started to yell and scream, "Why now? Why now? This is so unfair. He was just about to get his wish. Why now? Why now?"

Nurse Sarah

Sarah said, with a calm empathetic tone, "I am sorry. I am so sorry for your lost." Sarah spoke with considerable care. She did not want to add insult to injury, so she said, "Ma'am."

Cindy said, still crying, "My name is Cindy. Could you please just call me Cindy."

Sarah quickly obliged and said, "Sure. Cindy, did your husband have some health issues or something?"

"No," Cindy replied, "I just found out that I am pregnant. He was on his way home and I was going to surprise him with the news. He finally got his wish. He was going to be a father. All he ever wanted was to be a husband and father. This is so unfair." Cindy cried.

"I am sorry. I am truly sorry."

"Does anyone know what happened?" Cindy asked.

"From what we can gather, it was a hit and run. No witnesses. It appears from the way he was found that he never saw what hit him," Sarah replied.

"Where did this happen?" inquired Cindy.

"The paramedics reported that he was found in the street near the Shopping Square. There was a pint of strawberry mint cheesecake ice cream from the local creamery not too far from where his body was found."

Cindy started crying even more.

"Cindy, I am so sorry. I did not want to tell you this over the phone. I wanted to meet you, to ensure you were in a safe place when you heard. This is the toughest part of my job. I know you don't know me, but you seem like a nice person and I wish we could have met under better circumstances. I never like telling folks that someone they loved has been killed or has passed away, especially over the phone. I find it to be cold and uncaring so that's why I insisted you come down to the Hospital."

Cindy had her head in her hands, still crying. She looked up and said, "Yeah, thank you for that."

"I hope you don't mind me asking, but how far along are you?"

"I am not sure. I just took the home pregnancy test this morning, and it was positive."

"Do you have a primary care physician at this hospital?"

"Yes, Dr. Wendy Samuel."

"I know Dr. Samuel. Would you like me to schedule an appointment for you to see her as soon as her schedule allows?"

"Sure, that would be fine. I don't know what I am going to do. I am all alone yet again."

"Do you have any family?"

"No, RJ was my family and now I am all alone, yet again."

"Again?"

"Yes," Cindy snapped, "My parents were killed in a freak accident when I was 25. They were on vacation in Brazil, when the hotel they were staying at fell into a sinkhole. My parents along with 100 others lost their lives. I was just getting home for summer break from college." Cindy was awarded a full-ride scholarship to Julliard for singing and music composing. "When I got the call, I had just arrived at my house. All I can remember was the person telling me my parents are dead. Then later I found out they fell into a hole or the hotel fell into one. It happened in the middle of the night so they probably never knew what happened. It seems my life is laced with sudden death."

Cindy apologized to Sarah for being snappy. "I am just so angry, scared and frustrated. I am 35 years old and pregnant, no family to speak of and my husband is dead. I am all alone. What am I to do? God, why are You doing this to me? Why me, Lord? Why me? I thought You were love and all that jazz. This does not feel like love to me, God. Not at all. God, where are You? Why did You let this happen? Why, Lord, why?" Cindy began crying more.

Cindy's Conversion

Cindy began sobbing all over again. Sarah placed her arm on her shoulder and leaned in to tell her that she was not alone. Cindy said, "Maybe not now, but what happens tomorrow or the next day?"

"I am not talking about me, I am talking about God and His Son, Jesus, who died on the cross for you and me. The One you were just yelling at and asking questions about all of this."

Cindy was spiritual, not one for religion, but she did believe in God and she was aware of Jesus as being His only begotten Son, but not much more than that. Cindy stopped going to Church after she went off to College. She blamed God for her brother's death and her parents.

Cindy said, "God doesn't care about things like this anyway. He is only concerned with major things."

Sarah looked confused and responded, "Don't you think having a child and no father is major?"

"I don't think this qualifies as major. He didn't stop my brother from dying at nine or kept my parents alive in Brazil. I don't think this qualifies as major on His to-do list."

"I get it. You're hurt and angry at God and you think He has abandoned you. I know, I felt the same way when my life fell apart a while ago. I felt angry, frustrated and lied to about this all-loving God who would allow me to have to deal with all this pain."

Cindy, still crying, asked, "What happened?"

"We were on vacation, my husband and I and our three children in Brazil ten years ago. We were in the hotel across from the one that fell into the hole. To make a long story short, I am the only one who returned home from vacation. My husband and children went to visit his sister and brother in-law that night in the hotel that fell in the hole. So I know a little bit about how you may be feeling."

"How did you get through it?"

"I turned to God and asked Him to help me. I attempted suicide by taking some pills and, for some reason, I didn't die; I just had a terrible stomach ache. I was yelling at God, telling Him to let me die. At that moment, I heard a voice say, 'You have more to do. Your life has meaning and I have a great plan for you. Do you want what I have for you?' I felt so loved and at complete peace in that moment. I cried out, 'Yes, I want what You have, God. Help me, Lord. Help me get through this.'"

Sarah paused and looked at Cindy and asked, "Do you want help? Do you think you can trust God to get you through this?"

Cindy nodded her head as she was still sobbing in a low simmer. Sarah asked, "Would you like to have God's help in this situation and all the others that will arise with you and your new baby?"

Cindy said, "Yes. Yes, I need something. It hurts so bad, I am so scared. I don't know what I am going to do."

Sarah said, "I get it, I have been there before: scared, angry and full of frustration. I know it doesn't feel like it now, but God is with you even now. He wants to help you carry this, could you please repeat after me..."

Cindy agreed and Sarah led her to the Lord. "Heavenly Father, I know I am a sinner and I have fallen short of your glory. I repent from my life of sin and accept your Son, Jesus Christ, as my Lord and Savior. I know He died on the cross that I may live. Jesus, please save me and live with me and help me in every area of my life, in Jesus name I pray. Amen." Cindy said the prayer and was saved.

Sarah asked, "Do you believe that you are saved?"

"I don't know. I don't feel too much different, maybe a little lighter, but that's about it."

"That's normal. The more you study and develop a relationship with God, Jesus, and the Holy Spirit, the more you will realize what it means to be saved by grace…"

"The Holy what?" Cindy inquired.

"The Holy Spirit," replied Sarah. "It is where God will come live on the inside of you. You will never be alone again."

"Oh, okay. Holy Spirit, Holy Spirit," Cindy repeated.

Sarah asked, "Is this the first time you heard about the Holy Spirit?"

"Yeah, no, I mean, I heard the term but I never believed or understood what it was all about."

"The Holy Spirit will bring you into all knowledge and truth. It is the Spirit of God living on the inside of you. He will guide you, teach you and bring you through any and all trials, if you listen to Him. Do you have a Bible?"

"I think so, but I am not sure where it is at the moment."

"Would you like another one?"

"Yes, I would."

"Hold on. Please wait right here for a moment and I will get one for you."

"Sure. Where am I going to go!"

Sarah walked down the hall and slowly faded from sight. Cindy sat alone in the emergency waiting room, not truly alone, but alone in her mind. Cindy looked up and spoke with pain in her voice, "Why did You take them from me? Why? All I ever wanted was to give him what he wanted, a child, and You took him before he could enjoy it. Why, God? Why would You do this?"

Cindy heard a voice that sounded like RJ, with his smooth baritone voice, "Cindy, I know you are hurting, but this baby will be a gift to you and the world. Don't do anything to him or yourself. He is My gift to you."

"RJ, where are you? RJ, RJ, RJ, where are you?"

"I am not RJ," the voice replied.

"Then who are You?"

"I Am that I Am. I Am here with you and will never leave you. Trust me, I am always here. I AM always working everything out for your good. I know it doesn't seem fair, but I am doing what is best for you and the purpose I have for you and your son. My ways are not your ways; the way you think it should go, is not how I planned it. I designed life to be just, not fair. Trust me, I love you and I am always here with you. You will never be alone. I will be there going through the pain with you."

It was the Lord telling Cindy that she was carrying a gift. She did not know how special her baby would become.

Sarah returned with a Bible and some Scriptures highlighted: Psalms 23 and Ephesians 4:9-17. She said, "Start with these, if you feel like you don't know where to begin."

"Okay, and thank you."

A Child Is Born

While on a short tour in Memphis, TN, Cindy had her baby; a healthy baby boy. The nurses and the doctor wondered what the child's name would be. "What are you going to name him?"

"I will need to think about it. Give me till tomorrow."

That night, Cindy just stared at the little boy. She looked at him as if to ask him his name. She thought, "What's your name going to be? Who are you, little guy?" In that moment, Cindy said out loud: "I know your name. It is Johnathon Jason Jones. That is who you are, Johnathon Jason Jones, a gift from your Father."

After she was released from the hospital, she returned to Houston Suburbs in Texas, where she and RJ lived for the past few years. Cindy taught Johnathon about God, music, and science. She taught him that he was a gift from his Father. She always told him that he was her great gift.

Cindy went back to singing, writing and performing all over the world. She brought Johnathon with her. One day, she was performing in Italy at the largest Jazz festival in Europe. Minutes before she went on stage, she felt a sharp pain in her chest. She thought she was having a heart attack. Cindy panicked before realizing that one of the wires in her bra came loose and was poking her in her chest right above her heart. She put on another bra and said to herself, "I have to see if I can find any family members for RJ. There has to be someone that can care for Johnathon in the event of my death."

Lesson In The Story

Despite his effect on women, Ross was a perfect gentleman. He often said, "I will never understand why women react that way." Ross was no fool; he used it to book more gigs. Ross never used his gift to take advantage of anyone.

Because you don't understand why you have favor, does not mean you should not use it. Don't be afraid to let love in. Cindy was afraid to let RJ love her because she had a rare heart condition. RJ knew he wanted to marry her, even when she didn't know it. Don't waste time running from the blessings placed right in front of you because you are afraid of what could happen. Cindy, even though she eventually said yes, wasted time running from her blessings because she was afraid. When you see your blessing in front of you, don't run from it, instead run toward it. You don't know how much time you will have with the blessing. Remember life is not coincidental; everything happens for a reason. Because you can't see the why, doesn't mean there isn't one. Sarah came into Cindy's life for a reason: to introduce her to God. Some people are temporary, others are there for a lifetime. Do not confuse temporary people with lifetime ones. The most important lesson is that even when you don't feel it, God is with you. He sees it all. He is right there with you all the time, working out all of the kinks and ironing out the wrinkles of life to make it better for you.

Chapter 5
THE SEARCH FOR FAMILY

Cindy went on a quest to find any living relative that would be willing to care for her gift of a son, Johnathon. She found a uncle of RJ named Buck Bartholomew Jones. He lived in Texas in the hill country outside of Austin. He had a nice piece of property there, about 160 acres of land that he used to raise grass-fed cattle. Buck was surprised when Cindy called. He heard nothing of his brother having a child before he died in a plane crash almost thirty years prior.

Buck offered for Cindy to come out to the ranch whenever she was in town. Cindy was touring, writing and composing all over the world. So she only made it to the ranch once or twice, however, they kept in contact over the years. The first time she visited the ranch, 3-Jay was only one year old. Buck's wife died a few years later and he was feeling lonely, so he was looking forward to seeing Cindy and Johnathon again. The next time she visited, 3-Jay was seven; just one year after Buck's wife had passed.

Enter Buck Jones A.K.A. Mr. B

Buck was known in the community as Mr.B, the sweet, honest rancher. Mr. B was sixty-seven years old at the time of his wife's death, but he looked and acted like a strong 40-year-old. No one had a clue that Mr. B was in his late 60s. He did not have any children of his own, so he had a fondness for them but was a little rough around the edges in his approach to them; most children feared him, until they got to know him.

One day, after Cindy's 45th birthday, she died from that dreaded rare heart condition that took her brother, Charles. She was just finishing up a song she had written for Johnathon sitting at the piano when she fell over and died. Cindy had left explicit instructions for Johnathon to go live with Mr. B in the event of her death. Johnathon was ten years old when his mother died. He went to live with Mr. B. Cindy had saved up some money to help care for Johnathon, about $500,000. Mr. B was not in any need of money, so he left the money in a trust account that Johnathon could not touch until he turned twenty-five years old.

Three years prior, when Cindy was in Europe, she was telling Johnathon about her heart condition. She told him before, but she was very insistent that he understood that at any moment she could die without cause. She wanted him to be prepared for that moment. Johnathon, being a gifted child, polite and respectful, said, "I understand, mom."

She said, "Johnathon, remember who you are. Life happens. You need to remember who you are when it does. Don't let events or circumstances cause you to forget who you are. No matter what life throws at you, remember who you are. You are a gift from your Father."

"Momma, I know I am Johnathon Jason Jones, a gift from my father, yeah, yeah, I know you have been telling me this all my life. Why do you keep telling me this anyway?"

"I don't want you to ever forget that you are a gift from your Father to me and the world. Life can be a hard task-master, and double for anyone who don't know who they are. Never forget, you are a gift from your Father."

"Fine." 3-Jay responded in a way to just appease his mom and shut her up. He never really took what she said to heart, but in time it would all come back to him.

3-Jay went to live with Mr. B in the hill country of Texas outside of Austin. Mr. B was a huge football fan, just like everyone else in Texas. Mr. B was a successful rancher, who had been raising grass-fed beef before it was popular. He was never one to mince words and always said what he meant with little regard to how it sounded. He was never mean, cruel or intentional on hurting someone's feeling. He was direct, brutally honest, gruff and unfiltered.

Mr. B was well-liked, once people got past his unashamed honest nature. He never lied; always told the truth, even if it hurt him. Don't get me wrong, Mr. B had other issues, just like everyone else. He was competitive and hated to lose control of anything, especially his own emotions, so he rarely showed how deep things affected him. He was calm, cool and was never rattled by much of anything.

When 3-Jay came to live with him, Mr. B was over the moon, but it showed little, if any, on his face. Now remember, Mr. B was a huge football fan, so he imagined that 3-Jay would be a big football fan, player or, at least, interested in the game. When 3-Jay arrived, he was a tall, stocky boy, who looked like he could play tight-end or be a good wide receiver, but he was not the least bit interested in football or any sports for that matter.

When Mr. B saw 3-Jay, he said, "Man, you have grown so much in three years. What position do you play son?"

3-Jay responded, a bit confused, "What position? I play sitting down most of the time." 3-Jay thought he was talking about how he played his saxophone or flute, not knowing that Mr. B was talking about football.

Mr. B remarked, "Sitting down? With your size? You a benchwarmer? You don't get any game time?"

3-Jay realized at that moment what he was asking. He laughed and said, "I don't play sports none at all."

"Not even football?"

"That's right, sir. I don't play any sports with mom traveling all over the world performing, singing and writing. I had little time to learn, so I grew disinterested over time. So, no football for me, sir. Thank you again for allowing me to stay here."

Mr. B was greatly disappointed that 3-Jay, who looked like he could play football, did not and, worst of all, was not even interested in learning. Mr. B felt disappointed. He said, in his direct but gruff tone, "Don't mention it. You're always welcome here." Mr. B walked away and began to reminisce about his wife.

Mr. B loved children, but all children did not love him since he was so direct and showed little in the realm of nurture when it came to dealing with little ones. Mr. B's philosophy when it came to children was, "Not because they small, don't mean they don't understand. Tell it to them straight. They will get it." Mr. B always wanted a lot of children, but he and his late wife could not have any. It was not for a lack of trying, that is for sure. They tried it all and spent an obscene amount of money to no avail; no children for them. His wife died some eleven years prior, so it was Mr. B, his ranch and soon it would be 3-Jay.

Mr. B was known as the gentle teddy bear who looked mean, spoke sharp, but would give the very shirt off his back, literally. About twenty years prior, a young farm-hand came to town looking for work. He had nothing of value to speak of. Mr. B saw him in town asking for money to buy a new shirt, since he just found some work at a small cattle ranch on the outskirts of town. Mr. B asked him what he did and why he did not have a shirt. The young farm-hand told Mr. B his sad story of why he was homeless, wandering South Texas looking for work. Mr. B listened attentively to every word, and then said, "So you need a new shirt for work?"

"Yes, sir. That's correct."

Mr. B said nothing more. He started to take off his shirt. The young man said, "What are you doing?"

Mr. B said nothing for what felt like an eternity to the young man. Then he responded, "I am giving you a new shirt. I just bought this shirt not less than a week ago. This situation calls for me to give it to you. See, this is the only time I have worn this shirt. So here you go."

The young man said, "Thank you, sir. Thank you so very much. I won't forget you for this kindness."

"Don't mention it. Really, don't mention it."

The young man went off to his business, and Mr. B saw his wife smiling in sheer delight. Mr. B loved to see her smile.

"What are you smiling at, lady?"

"You, Mr. Jones. I am smiling at the kindest man I know, who gave a stranger a brand new shirt off his back. That is why I married you. You are rough around the edges, but you have a heart of gold and that's just the truth of the matter."

Mr. B smiled, and they went on their way.

Intermission In The Story

We all ask these questions, "Who am I? Where did I come from? Why am I here?"

I want to answer these questions and a few more as we go through this book. Many of us assume our identity from our parents, family and culture. We respond to names as if they could accurately describe who we are. We use names like Black, White, French, Mexican, Hispanic, Native American or Asian. These names do not, and cannot, tell us who we are. All they do is tell us where we came from or the culture we were born into. They have nothing to do with who we are.

Some of us use our occupation to describe who we are. We say things like, "I am a teacher, a fire fighter, doctor, lawyer or IT professional, etc." None of these titles define who we are. They describe what field we operate in to make money.

When someone ask you who you are, they are not asking what you do. They are asking you a much deeper question. They want to know your story. The problem with this question is that most of us don't have an adequate answer. We don't know who we are. So, this is why we use culture, occupation and club affiliation to answer that question of who we are. Truth is, most of us don't know who we are. We are clueless to who we are, so we let what we do or the culture we grew up in to define us. You are not a single cell organism, we are multi-faceted with peaks and valleys in our make-up. We are not one thing, but a composite of many.

Think for a moment. Consider that you are so many things that one word could not actually tell them who you are. We, as people, are not one, but many. People try to put us in a group, box, hole or category that best suits them. We don't fit so nicely in boxes, but that doesn't stop people from putting us in them.

Back to our question, "Who are you?" For such a short question, it takes a lot of words to answer. I don't know where to begin to answer that question without explaining to you who our Father is. I will suspend that explanation for now; let us get back to our story.

3-Jay Hears Voices

3-Jay was now living with Mr. B on the ranch, learning about cattle, longhorns and horses. He was finally starting to feel better. 3-Jay came into the house one day, after being out in the field with Mr. B. As he walked through the door, he had a memory of his mom singing to him. He paused and looked up in wonderment. Mr. B asked, "What's wrong, 3-Jay? It looks like you are lost in deep thought?"

"No, I am fine. Nothing is wrong. I will be alright."

Mr. B was keen on words and body language. He said, "Which is it son? Are you fine or will you be alright? Something is going on. What is it?"

3-Jay was embarrassed as he spoke, "I hear my mom singing to me. Crazy, right?"

Mr. B grabbed 3-Jay and pulled him closer and said, "Listen to me, that is not crazy. That is how God let's you know that He has not forgotten about you."

3-Jay was confused and said, "What does God have to do with my mom singing?"

"How do you feel?"

"Warm, loved, and lonely all at the same time."

"That warm love you feel is God hugging you through the memory of your mom singing. The loneliness is your memory missing your mom. Don't forget that whenever you hear your mom singing to you, it is really God reaching out of heaven to give you a hug and say, 'I am here with you.' God loves us so much. He is a good Father, and even though we can't see Him, He often sends us love notes through memories and warm feelings to remind us that He is here with us. 3-Jay, I need you to remember what I am telling you. You're not crazy and know that God will never leave you. Will you remember this? I am serious, you must remember."

"Okay, I will."

3-Jay was still not convinced that God was hugging him but he learned early not to argue and just listen and see what happens. He went into the house and headed towards the kitchen to grab a bite to eat. At that moment, he heard his name, "Johnathon, remember. Johnathon, remember."

"Mr. B, did you call me?"

"No," replied Mr. B. "Why?"

"Oh, nothing, I just thought you did."

3-Jay went back to forging for food. He heard it again; same voice, same words. He said, "Remember what? Who is this?"

"Remember who you are," the voice responded.

"Yeah, sure. Please stop talking. I am looking for something to eat. I don't have time for this."

He kept looking for something to eat. The voice got louder and he heard his mom singing to him as well. 3-Jay said, "God?"

There was no response. 3-Jay dismissed it as he was very hungry. Then he heard his mom singing again and the voice saying, "Remember who you are." 3-Jay started to get angry and said, "This is not funny. This is weird. Who are you, and why are you doing this?"

At that moment Mr. B walked in and said, "3-Jay, what's going on? Why are you yelling?"

"I am not yelling. I am just tired of hearing voices. I think I am going crazy."

"Hold on a minute, take a breath. What voices are you hearing?"

"I keep hearing my mom singing and the words, 'Remember who you are.'"

Mr. B smiled and said, "3-Jay, you are not losing your mind and you are not crazy. God is trying to get your attention."

"I asked if it was God, and everything went silent, so I don't think it was God. I think I may be losing my mind. I know something is wrong with me."

"Come here, 3-Jay. Listen to me, you are not going crazy and nothing is wrong with you. Who told you something was wrong with you? Who said you were crazy?" Mr. B looked him in the eye and asked again, "Who told you that?"

"No one. I just know it."

"Boy, you don't know nothing when it comes to who you are. You are not crazy and nothing is wrong with you. God made you just like He wanted. You are special and God is calling you for something. I don't know what it is, but listen to Him and seek to understand it. Whatever it is, it is very important and that is why He is getting your attention now."

"Okay, but something is wrong with me. I just know it."

"Nothing is wrong with you. Trust me, nothing is wrong with you. God has a call on your life and He don't make no mistakes. God said you are good; believe it and leave it. You think you know better than God? Do you think you know more than me when it comes to you being good, crazy or anything?"

"No, sir."

"Why are we having this discussion about something being wrong with you? I told you and your mom told you. You're a gift, and God loves you. God is reaching down from heaven to tell you the same thing. Why do you doubt that you are a gift and have something special to offer?"

Who Am I?

The voice came back, "Remember who you are."

"Who am I? Who am I? Tell me. I don't know." 3-Jay broke down in tears. Mr. B grabbed him, hugged him and said, "You are loved. You are okay. Let it out. I know you miss your mom. It's only been a few months since you arrived."

3-Jay was sobbing, and asking, "Who am I? Who am I? I can't remember who I am. I don't know who I am. I don't know." Mr. B hugged him and said nothing.

3-Jay tried to push Mr. B away but Mr. B hung on to him and said, "I am not going anywhere. I am here for you. Let it out. Tonight when you pray, ask God that exact question, 'Who am I.'"

"I don't know how to do that."

"Just ask Him. He is a loving Father. He will listen and respond to you in His own way, you just have to ask."

"I will. I will ask Him." 3-Jay said, still crying.

That night, before 3-Jay went to sleep, he looked out the window and up at the sky and said, "God, who am I?" He heard nothing. "God, are you awake?" Nothing. "God, please tell me who I am?" Nothing. He got into bed and gazed at the ceiling for what seemed like hours, but it was only about twenty minutes. 3-Jay was laying there, frustrated and still looking at the ceiling, while asking in his mind, "Who am I? Who am I? Who am I?"

The voice came back, riding on the singing of his mother, "You are special. You are My gift to the world. I gave you life so you could give life through your life. You have more to offer than you know. Don't forget who you are. Remember who you are. Remember why you are." 3-Jay then drifted off to sleep.

Tragedy Strikes, Yet Again

3-Jay had been on the ranch living and learning from Mr. B, who had become the father he never had. 3-Jay was the son Mr. B longed to have. One day, 3-Jay was singing in the field and Mr. B heard him sing for the second time in five years. He called to 3-Jay, "3-Jay, come here." 3-Jay came running. He reached the edge of the gate where Mr. B was standing, a little out of breath. He bent over trying to catch his breath, "Yes, sir. Do you need me to do something else."

"Yes," Mr. B said, "I need you to keep doing that. Keep using your voice, keep playing your music."

3-Jay looked confused, and thought to himself, *"How did he know I could sing? I was so careful to keep it secret."*

"I heard you singing and what a voice. What a voice! You brought tears to my eyes."

3-Jay knew that was a big deal because Mr. B never expressed how he truly felt about anything. He was always so direct and stoic.

"Promise me, no matter what, you will keep singing and sharing your gift."

3-Jay felt a little embarrassed, "Sir, I wasn't really sharing my voice. I was just singing to the Lord. It was a private moment and now I feel like you were snooping around on me."

Mr. B said, with a smile, "Everyone within two counties could hear you. What a beautiful voice."

3-Jay was thinking, *I was not even singing loud. How could they hear me?*"

Mr. B said, "Don't stop singing. You have such a voice and that song you were singing, I never heard that one before."

"It was something I was working on."

"It's a great song, very moving. I enjoyed it. That's what I wanted to tell you. Keep singing, playing music and doing what you do. Remember who you are 3-Jay. Remember why you are here. Never forget who you are." Mr. B turned and walked away.

A few months later, 3-Jay was in the living room playing the piano. Mr. B was sitting in his favorite chair listening to 3-Jay. Mr. B said, "Can you play, 'When The Saints Go Marching In, 3-Jay style?'"

3-Jay had taken that song and rearranged it into a Jazzy hip-hop version that was unique and moving. As he played the music, Mr. B was enjoying the song. He laid back, closed his eyes and died. 3-Jay finished the song and was feeling it. He looked over at Mr. B and said, "How was that?" No response. 3-Jay got up and ran over to Mr. B and said, "Wake up!" He touched his hand trying to find a pulse and realized that Mr. B was dead. He called 911 and said, "My Uncle has stopped breathing. Send someone quick." He hang up the phone and began administering CPR. He was still administering it when the EMT's showed up some 10-15 minutes later. When the EMT's arrived, they asked 3-Jay how long he had been doing CPR. 3-Jay said, "I don't know. I started after I got off the phone with 911." The EMT's looked at each other and said, "Son, let us take over." They began to administer CPR, but they knew that Mr. B was dead. They took him to the hospital and pronounced him dead on arrival.

3-Jay felt anxious walking through the hall when he heard the devastating news: Mr. B had died. 3-Jay ran out of the hospital, angry and mad. He went back to the ranch, grabbed a bag that he brought with him five years before, looked at the ranch and walked out the door. He walked for about two miles, thought about the cattle, then turned back toward the ranch.

3-Jay worked the ranch for about a month before Child Protection Services (CPS) showed up to tell him he needed to go into Foster Care. He was only fifteen years old, so he could not stay on the ranch by himself. Even though he protested saying he had been there for a month, they told him it was against the law. "We are going to have to take you in with us."

3-Jay said, "No, I am not leaving my home. This is my home. I am not going nowhere." 3-Jay was only fifteen years old, but he was a tall, muscular boy who looked like a man from behind. The CPS worker became afraid and called the police. 3-Jay finally said, "Okay, I will go." He grabbed his bag and got into the car. He thought to himself, "As soon as I can, I am coming back home."

3-Jay was shipped to Houston due to overcrowding in the Austin Foster Care system.

A New Hope Of Something Better

Mr. B died and 3-Jay was now fifteen years old, homeless and in an unfamiliar territory, or so he thought. 3-Jay refused to stay in foster care, so he would always run away. The last foster home he was in was with an older couple. They knew that 3-Jay was not a bad kid, so they stopped reporting him the third time he ran away. They just told him that he could always come back when he wanted.

3-Jay was on the streets playing his saxophone for tips. He met a girl named Jordan. She was a smart, beautiful girl who dressed like she had no care in the world. She wore torn jeans and a grey t-shirt; her hair was wavy and natural, often tied in a pony tail. She walked past 3-Jay and asked him why he was on the street, "You don't look like you are homeless."

"I am not homeless. I am just not able to go home at the moment."

"Why?"

"Excuse me. You ask a lot of questions and I don't even know your name."

"My apologies. I am Jordan, you know, like Michael Jordan. My dad was a huge basketball fan."

"Who?"

"Don't tell me you don't know who the best basketball player of all time is. Where are you from? Have you been living under a rock?"

3-Jay knew who Michael Jordan was, but he wanted to keep talking to Jordan, so he played like he was not aware.

"What is your name anyway?"

"I am 3-Jay."

"How did you get that name?"

"There is a story, but I don't have time to tell you. If you meet me here tomorrow, maybe I will tell you."

"I will think about it. Bye, 3-Jay, maybe I will see you around."

Jordan walked off and 3-Jay was feeling all emotional about the encounter. Jordan was gorgeous even under all that unkempt looking mask. 3-Jay just knew it. 3-Jay did not see Jordan the next day or the day after that. He began to ask around about her. No one knew what had happened to her. Months passed and still no Jordan. Then, one day he was playing outside of a restaurant for tips, and out came this gorgeous girl who looked familiar, but he wasn't sure if it was her. He kept playing his saxophone. She was with two older folks who looked too young to be her parents, so he thought maybe they were a sister and brother.

The man walked over and gave 3-Jay a $5 tip and said, "Man, you play well."

The lady with him said, "If you can play this song, I will give you $20."

3-Jay said, "Okay." He knew there was not one song he could not play after hearing it. The lady played the song. It was his mother singing on the recording. 3-Jay froze for a moment and started to silently cry.

"What's the matter, young man?"

"Nothing."

3-Jay played the song and kept his head down the rest of the time with tears falling from his eyes.

Jordan noticed and asked, "3-Jay, what's the matter?"

"Nothing, nothing is wrong."

Jordan was not one to take no for an answer, "Then tell your eyes nothing is wrong, because you are crying."

"Why do you care? You disappeared. I have been looking for you for months. I thought you were homeless."

"I never said that."

"You looked homeless and everyone knew you and you knew I was new to the streets."

Jordan laughed, "I volunteer with my church youth group, working with homeless youth and runaways. I am not homeless. This is my mother and my step-d – dad, Mr. and Mrs. Wilson."

Mr. Wilson said, "Nice to meet you."

Mrs. Wilson asked, "What's wrong? Why did you start crying when I played that song?"

"It was one of my mother's favorite songs."

3-Jay did not tell them that the person singing was his mother.

Mrs. Wilson said, "I am sorry. What happened to your mother?"

"She died."

"I am sorry to hear that. Where are you staying?"

3-Jay gave the address for the old couple where he ran away from.

"Let us give you a ride back home."

"Sure, why not." He grabbed his stuff, got into the vehicle and rode back to town with them. While in the car, Jordan asked him if he would be interested in coming to a youth jam session at their church just thirty minutes north of downtown.

"What is a youth jam session?"

Jordan got all excited and said, "Once a month, our church allows all the youth to perform; singing, dancing, comedy, rap, spoken word, music and showcase three minute video shorts. There is just one rule: it must praise God or showcase God's love in some way."

"Maybe! When is it?"

"In about two weeks."

They talked some more. 3-Jay asked, "What will you do in this youth jam session, Jordan like in Michael?"

"Whatever I want," She said, smiling, "I organized it, but seriously, I will be singing or playing the piano."

"Really? You're going to sing? Can you sing?"

"Yes, I can sing. I can sing. Everyone can sing."

"True, but not everyone sounds good singing. If you can sing half as good as you look, I will be there."

"What did you say?"

3-Jay realized what he said, "If you can sing half as good as you look, I will be there."

"Okay, okay, I will sing, if you sing as well."

3-Jay had not sang anything since Mr. B passed away.

"Forget I said anything." 3-Jay said.

"Remember, anyone can sing. If it doesn't sound good, that doesn't matter, just be sincere."

"No, I am good."

"3-Jay, you're not going to sing at all? Why?"

"I just don't want to, okay." 3-Jay turned and started looking out the window. The rest of the ride was in silence.

Jordan was perplexed. She did not know how old 3-Jay was or his full story, but she wanted to know more. Jordan was feeling 3-Jay and, unknown to her, he was into her as well. Jordan was frustrated with what just happened, but not wanting to make matters worse, she just rode in silence wondering what just happened.

They dropped 3-Jay off at the Smith's house. He got out of the car and went into the house. The couple was sitting at the table having dinner.

"How long are you staying this time?"

"Not long. I will be out in the morning."

"You know you don't have to go."

Mrs. Smith loved children and was very kind. Mr. Smith was a good man as well. He was a lot like Mr. B and that was why 3-Jay refused to stay. He did not want to get close to them and something happened. He didn't think he could take it. Mr. Smith and Mr. B were old friends who lost contact when Mr. Smith went to the Air Force. He heard that Mr. B had died and he went to the funeral. He heard rumors that he had a nephew staying with him. No one had heard anything, so he called in some favors to get 3-Jay placed with them, hoping he could re-pay an old friend by taking care of his family.

3-Jay was on his way to his room and said, "Thank you for letting me, um, stay. Just, thank you." He went to his room and closed the door.

Mr. Smith said, "He will be okay. He has been through a lot."

Mrs. Smith responded, "I know. I wish he would talk to us and let us help him."

"In time, honey, in time. He will get tired of running away."

They finished their meal.

Out On The Town

3-Jay left the Smith's house and was out and about playing for tips as he had always done. He was at a new restaurant in the wealthy part of town playing for the patrons. Mr. and Mrs. Smith walked in and saw him playing. They didn't say anything. 3-Jay did not see them and they pretended like they did not see him. They ate their food and was trying to sneak out, when in walked Jordan with her mom. Jordan had a huge smile on her face, "Hello. You are Mr. and Mrs. Smith?"

"Yes, how did you know that?"

"3-Jay may have mentioned you a time or two."

"Are you here to see him play?" Mrs. Smith replied.

"No. Is he here?" Jordan inquired.

"Yes, he is over there getting ready to play again. We didn't want him to know we are here." Mr. Smith replied.

3-Jay was now seventeen and had been living on and off with the Smith's for the past two years. They developed a relationship, still distant, but a relationship none-the-less. 3-Jay was a handsome young man. He was a perfect blend of his mother and father. He had soft eyes, muscular build and a naturally deep speaking voice. He could hit high notes like he was soprano, but no one knew it.

Jordan said, "Excuse me. I am going to go say hello to 3-Jay."

3-Jay looked up and saw Jordan. She had blossomed into a gorgeous woman. She was nineteen years old, and was very curvy, like her mother.

"Hello, 3-Jay. It's been a while since I have seen you, almost six months. What have you been up to?"

"Umm, I, have been, um." He was at a loss for words. Jordan was breathtaking. All he could think to say was nothing. "I have been up to nothing."

"Nothing," she exclaimed, "Looks like you have been doing something. Here you are playing for tips at this upscale restaurant."

"Um, yeah, you, look - I mean, how have you been?"

Jordan smiled and said, "I have been doing good. Organizing and putting on Youth Jam Session. It's that time again."

"What time?"

"The youth jam session at my church. Are you going to come play for us? You said you would, but never did." Jordan said.

"Are you going to be there?" 3-Jay asked.

"Of course. I will be singing this year as well."

"Really? What song will you be singing?" 3-Jay inquired.

"A semi-original that I re-arranged, 'I Will Be Missing You by Sting.' I turned it into a gospel song."

"No kidding. You write songs?" 3-Jay was intrigued, Jordan reminded him a lot of his mother in that way. His mom was always writing and re-writing music. Taking country pop songs and turning them into Jazz ballad or whatever she felt like.

"A little. I just like sharing my gift with the world. 3-Jay, would you be willing to sing with me? I still haven't heard you sing." Jordan remarked.

"Yeah, I know."

Jordan's mind fell on that moment when she asked him to sing with her and he went silent. "Are you sure? You don't have to sing. I will sing. Will you just play for me?"

"Sure, I'm sure. I will sing with you."

3-Jay started playing 'I Will Be Missing You' on the acoustic guitar. Jordan closed her eyes, grabbed the mic and started singing her version of the song. 3-Jay was amazed at how crisp her voice was; it had music in it. He was in awe and had stopped playing. No one seemed to notice; her voice was just that beautiful. She finished the song with 3-Jay just holding his guitar, mouth wide open and the restaurant cheering. She was totally unaware of the crowd; she was lost in the song.

"Thank you for playing with me. Will you be at the jam session this Saturday?"

"Yes, yes, I will be there." 3-Jay was excited and didn't realize how excited he was.

Jordan said, "Okay, Mr. Excitement. Will you be performing though?"

"Yes, I will play the piano, if you sing another song that you have written." 3-Jay remarked trying to maintain his cool since Jordan busted him out on how excited he was.

"Okay, it's a date. I mean, see you soon.... Um, this Saturday."

Jordan smiled and began to walk back towards her mother. 3-Jay watched her walk over to her mother and saw Mr. and Mrs. Smith. He waved to them and continued playing. He smiled and they smiled backed. Mr. Smith said, "Mrs Smith, our boy got the bug."

"What bug?"

"He is in love and don't even know it. Jordan has caught his eye."

She smiled, "And just like that, I caught your eye all them years ago."

"Yep, just like that. 3-Jay don't know it, but he is in love."

3-Jay showed up at the church early to set-up and see what it looked like. The youth pastor, Jeremy, was there setting up extra chairs and putting out refreshments. He walked over to 3-Jay and said, "Welcome. I don't believe we have had the pleasure of meeting. I am the Youth Pastor here. My name is Jeremy." He extended his hand.

"My name is 3-Jay." They shook hands.

Jeremy looked at him with curiosity. 3-Jay noticed and said, "That's what everyone calls me. I am Johnathon Jason Jones."

"Oh, 3-Jay. Yeah." They both laughed. "Well, 3-Jay, how did you hear about our event?"

"Jordan told me about it."

"Oh, you go to school with Jordan?"

"No, I just know her from doing music."

"Oh, you're a musician?"

"If you want to call it that. I just use music to make money and to relax. I am not that good."

"I see. Are you just saying that or have you been told that?"

"I dunno. I guess I am saying it. People don't usually say anything, they just look and maybe clap."

Pastor Jeremy was a huge music lover, and he was curious to see what 3-Jay could do. "Do you mind playing something for me?"

"Like what?"

"Anything you like."

"Okay." 3-Jay walked over to the piano and started playing his version of 'When The Saints Go Marching In' and he started singing as well. He got lost in the song, and went all in. Everyone in the church stopped and listened. When he finished, everyone was silent with tears streaming down their faces. Pastor Jeremy said, "That was amazing. 3-Jay, you have a real gift. You have something special. Did you write that?"

"Yeah. You know, this is the first time I have sang this song since my uncle died. I am not even sure why I chose it. It just felt right."

Jeremey asked, "How long ago did your Uncle pass?"

"It's been almost two and a half years now. It seems like yesterday."

"Did he teach you how to sing, and play music?"

"No, it has been something I could just do. I guess you can say my mother taught me."

"You have such range and control. Did you have any training?"

"None, other than from my mother."

"Wow, you got some skills."

"Thanks."

3-Jay knew he was good, but he was not very confident in his abilities.

Pastor Jeremy said, "Thank you for allowing me to enjoy your gift. It was a pleasure. I have to go finish setting up. You can wait around here until we get started. I will see you later." Pastor Jeremy walked away and 3-Jay was left standing and looking off into space toward the stage.

A while later, Jordan walked up behind 3-Jay. She stood there for about a minute before 3-Jay realized she was there. He turned to look around and bumped into her. "Excuse me. Where did you come from?"

She started laughing, "I have been standing here for a while, at least a minute. Where were you? You had this look of disbelief on your face."

"I was just thinking of my mom, Mr. B and why I am here and they are not."

"Wow, that's deep and a little sad. Are you alright?"

"Yeah, I am good."

The Youth Jam

The youth jam went from a mild jam session and turned into an all out revival. There were children who started preaching, singing and worshipping. 3-Jay was the next one to go on. He froze, "I am not sure I can do this."

Pastor Jeremy said, "What's wrong, 3-Jay?"

"This is too much. How am I to go out there, after all of that?"

Jordan came up to him and said, "I will be there with you."

"I know, I know, but I am not like you all."

"What do you mean not like us?"

"I am not saved. I am not - that good."

Pastor Jeremy interjected, "What do you mean you're not that good? I heard you and you are awesome. You have some real skills. Your voice is like butter; it is so smooth – you have range."

Jordan interrupted, "Excuse me, Pastor, you said you heard him sing?" She turned to 3-Jay, "Why haven't I heard you sing?"

"Um, I don't know. You just haven't."

Pastor Jeremy said, "Looks like you have been hiding for a while, 3-Jay. Would you like to be free and let loose and pour out all your pain in your gift?"

"Yes," 3-Jay said hesitantly, "But I am not sure I can."

Pastor Jeremy said, "You won't have to do it alone. Let the Holy Spirit guide you."

"Holy what?"

"The Holy Spirit; God in Spirit form who leads us all into every good thing in this life."

3-Jay's Awakening

Pastor Jeremy led 3-Jay in a prayer to accept and trust God for all he needed and never to lean on his own understanding; to believe that Jesus is the Son of God, who died and rose again on the third day as a Redeemer to save the lost and dying in the world. Pastor Jeremy looked at 3-Jay and said, "Welcome to the family; the body of Christ. You are now saved."

"I did this with my mom when she was alive. I just thought it was something to do. We travelled so much, I never really had a chance to get to know what salvation was all about. She told me things like, 'Remember who you are. Never forget you are a gift from your Father to the world.' I thought she was talking about my biological father. I just realized she was talking about God. Why couldn't she just say that, it may have helped."

Pastor Jeremy said, "Maybe she thought it was better for you to discover it for yourself. If you don't mind me asking, what happened to your mom and dad?"

"No, I don't mind. My mom died about seven years ago of a rare heart disease. I never knew my dad. He died before I was born. My mom said he was struck by a vehicle and died on the spot."

"What was your mother's name?"

"Cindy Jones and my father was Ross, but everyone called him RJ."

"Wait. I think I knew or at least met your parents. My cousin was very close to them both. He should be here tonight. After the event, please wait around so I can connect you two."

"Okay, sure. I will."

Jordan said, "We have to go on. The crowd looks like they are getting a little restless."

Jordan walked out and looked back for 3-Jay, but he did not come from behind the curtain. She looked again and still no 3-Jay. She grabbed the mic and started to hum one of her original songs. She heard a saxophone hum in tune with her. It was 3-Jay playing the sax. She started singing and he played right along with her, like they had rehearsed it. The crowd was hooked; no one said a word, except for the occasional, "Go, you got this." Jordan turned to look at 3-Jay. He mouthed to her, "I think I am ready."

"For what?"

She started singing the bridge and he played right along. She finished the song and the place erupted with applause. He leaned over and whispered in her ear, "To let you hear me sing."

She smiled and said, "Ladies and gentlemen, we have a special treat for you. My friend on the sax would like to sing a song for you. I hear he has a great voice, but I will let you all be the judge of that. Please give a warm welcome to 3-Jay."

3-Jay opened his mouth and sang his rendition of "Stairway to Heaven." There was not a dry eye in the house. Jordan was in awe. She could not believe what she was hearing. After 3-Jay finished singing, it was silent for a moment. 3-Jay thought it was because he was not good, then they all stood on their feet and applauded. He was finally free; he found his voice. He knew who he was in that moment. He was a gift, that had a gift, that needed to be shared. Jordan came back on the stage and gave him a big hug and said, "You were holding out on me. Why?"

He said, "I never thought I was any good."

Jordan smiled and said, "Boy, you are more than good. You are truly gifted."

3-Jay said, "I believe you. I heard you sing so I figure you have to know what you're talking about."

They took a bow and walked off the stage. Pastor Jeremy called for them to come over and meet his cousin JJ. JJ was crying, tears were rolling down his face. He grabbed 3-Jay, hugged him and said, "You remind me so much of your father. We were best friends. Your mother was like my sister."

3-Jay looked at him closely and remembered him, "Uncle JJ! It has been a while. The last time I saw you I was eight."

JJ responded, "After your mom passed away, I looked for you. I did, but no one seemed to know anything."

They spent the rest of the day talking and sharing stories. 3-Jay told JJ about Mr. B and JJ told him how his parents met and how he and his dad were best of friends.

The Lesson

From the story above, we can see that our main character, 3-Jay, had some challenges and false identity. He did not know who he was. This loss/false identity left him confused and feeling out of place. He was really no different from any one of us. We all have fallen victim to a false view of who we are. Even when those close to us tried to tell us, we often looked outward before we ever look within to discover who we are.

We can all relate to our natural parents or, at least, acknowledge that they help to shape our identity or the lack thereof. All of us draw a little, if not most, of who we are based on who they are and what kind of background they may have come from. We may know our grandparent's names and some of us know our great grandparents; that is good, but how many of us know the names of our heavenly Father? How much do we know about our Father God? Do we even want to know

Him personally? Do we think it is even possible to know Him like we know another person? Do we know that He always was, and He is Love? Do we know that we are, because He gave up His only begotten Son so we could have life? Did you know that He is the full embodiment of the fruit of the Spirit? Did you know that He loves you more than words could express? See, when I am asked who am I, my answer should be: "the righteousness of Christ; a son of the most high God," but it is not. I usually just give my name. That only tells the person how to address me; it says nothing about who I am.

The only reason any of us exists is because our Father came to the earth in the body of Jesus Christ. Religion would have us believe that Jesus was a deity and so far above us as common mankind. I have to disagree; He is our example of what a whole person can be. Please don't misunderstand me, I know He is God in the flesh, so yes, He is God and also man. Now here is where I may get some hate-mail from overzealous, under-informed religious people. We too are gods, not on the same level as the Father, but we are made in His image and likeness. We could not be made in the image and likeness of God and not be a god ourselves. I don't bring this up to cause confusion but to shed some light on the question of "Who am I?" 3-Jay heard his mother singing to him, and he sat up quickly and asked, "Who is that? Who is there?" Then he said, "I am here, Lord. Please tell me who I am?" He remembered his mother telling him that he is a gift to the world from his Father.

"Lord, am I a gift to the world?"

God's response, "Yes, and so much more. Remember, you have a purpose and you were sent with a gift for the world."

Chapter 6
I AM WHO I AM SAYS I AM

I am who I AM says I am. God, the Father, sent Jesus to redeem my sin-sick soul from death and eternal damnation. Jesus is my brother by adoption. I say, He is my brother by creation. Jesus was flesh and Spirit; we are flesh, blood and spirit. Our blood is what keeps us from being just like Jesus. This is why He had to shed His blood for our sake.

Our blood is tainted, dark and full of all kinds of wickedness. Our blood is what some call our flesh or fallen nature. We think of our physical body as our flesh, but that is not the whole story; our flesh is in our blood as well. It is our unchecked emotions that derive from what we sense in our body and is not to be confused with the emotions of our soul. Flesh is our emotions unchecked, out of control and following the rules of fear, instead of submitting to the Lord in truth and faith.

Our flesh is selfish, self-centered and self-focused, all day, everyday. It wants what it wants, not caring about what it needs for the long haul. We need blood to live; we need emotions to interact with people. Here is where we miss it: we assume that what we think, feel and see is the complete story: we feel it, we think it, so it must be what it is, and we take it as being right. In truth, it is utterly wrong or, at least, misdirected. We are not what we feel; we are who we call ourselves in our minds and say we are with our actions. What we say we are, we will become but that is not who we are at the core.

We are the righteousness of God, through Christ Jesus, if we accept Jesus as Lord. We are joint heirs with Jesus by faith, not by fear, not by how we feel, not by where we were born. We are His by faith, not by what we have done or will do. We are His by confessing with our mouth and believing in our hearts that we are saved, and that is how we go from darkness to light.

Our emotions is like the seasoning we use to enhance our food. Too much of it, and a good meal will quickly turn untasty. Not enough, and our food is bland and lacks flavor. It is all about balance. God gave us emotions so we can live life filled with great experiences, not so we are ruled and controlled by them.

If the body was the issue, then why was Jesus born of a woman? That whole process was how He got His body. Our body is a vehicle to transport us in this realm. We are not talking about simple ideas and basic religion, we are talking about truth, kingdom and relationship with the Father. We are talking about our true identity as a son of God. Your religion is not who you are. Some say they are a Christian, some Muslim, so on and so forth. These are all labels of religion, and none of them are true to who you are as a blood-washed son and daughter of God, our heavenly Father.

We can all agree that God is able to do whatever He wants; He is God. If he wanted us to be bound to religion, He would have come as a priest, pastor, preacher or teacher of the law, but He did not come that way. He came in the world as an underdog, from a ghetto called Nazareth. You are not where you were born. Jesus was born in a barn, amongst the animals. He hung out with what society would label as the lowest of the low: the tax collectors, harlots and fisherman; the ones most would overlook, discount or count out as unworthy. This is how Jesus came, so what makes you think your life must be a bed of thornless roses? What gives you the idea that you are only as good as the background you emerged from, that your history is your identity? Why do you believe these lies that you are who they say, and not who He says?

The reason I believe Jesus came in and through the process of man was to show us how a person connected to the Father could live. He is the perfect example of what it means to be a living, breathing, earth-walking child of God. We get our identity in Him; there is no other place we can point to for our true identity.

What do I mean when I say: "By creation we are gods?" Let me explain it in this matter: God, the Father, created us in His image and likeness. He gave us power over the earth and everything in the earth. He gave us the ability to call things into existence: whatever we call a thing, that is its name. We have the power, through Christ, to speak life and or death to any area in our lives.

We can speak to an inanimate object by faith, by God's proclamation, and they must obey us because God gave us dominion over all the earth (See Genesis 1:26).

God Created Us To Do What He Does

God created us to do what He does, but on a smaller scale. He allowed us to take part in creation by giving us the role to create things on the earth from things we found in the earth. We take this power of creation for granted. We call it several names: innovation, survival skills and, more currently, creativity. Let us look at the word "creativity." The root word is creative: the skill and ability to create something out of nothing or uncommon parts. God created us like Him, so we have the ability to create things like Him.

For every true identity comes a false one. The enemy, the fallen angel known in heaven as Lucifer, has fallen to earth, and we call him the devil. Some would have us believe that he is the yang to God's ying. This is not true; he is not of equal power to God. He is a fallen angel. God created him, so he cannot, and never will, be equal to God in any way. Does he have power? Yes, he does. His power is over the earth because our eldest brother, Adam, gave up the earth when he did not believe who God said He was. When God came in the body of Jesus, He reclaimed that power and gave it back to all who would allow Him to be head of their lives.

The devil is limited to the power we give him. He will never have more power than us, if we understand who we are in Christ Jesus and in the Kingdom of Heaven. However, if he can get us to doubt who we are, he can use our power against us. This is exactly what he does: he uses our power of thought and speech against us. This is how he does it: he throws thoughts of doubt, fear, shame and confusion out to the world. The world takes those thoughts, as if they created them and, therefore, act on them. Here is how we get all these wicked people doing evil things to one another: they forget who they are. They lost their identity; they have amnesia of sorts, and they think they are weak, when in reality, they are strong in Christ.

If you have amnesia, you must depend on someone else to tell you who you are, and the devil knows this, so he feeds us lies about who we are, what we want and what we can do. So many of us fall for the trickery and we end up breeding our children with the same form of amnesia. We are lost, not because we are not where we are supposed to be; we are lost, because we don't know who we are in the place we are, so we wander about aiming for self, when we should be reaching for the Father.

This is the program the devil has ran for thousands of generations and it works, and will continue to work, if we don't realize that "We are the children of God" and act accordingly. The enemy, the devil, is a great imposter. He is the father of lies, and those lies sound so good that we often take them as truth. When we take a lie as truth, it becomes a false truth (a stronghold) that holds us captive. Remember, whatever we call a thing, that is its name. We are lost people and we are looking for a place, a tribe and a people to call ours; someone we can identify with; a place we will know as home and then, maybe, we will know who we are. Our identity is not found in the external; our true identity was placed in us when we were born. It is a part of our internal; it is a part of our spiritual DNA.

We all have parents on the earth; those we are born to. Our parents may not be good parents or they could be great parents, if we compare them to the low standard of earthly parents. If we were to measure them to our Father, who is above the earth in heaven, we would soon see that even the best earth parent is nothing; they are wretched, broken and fearful shells filled with sin and shame. I know it sounds harsh, and some would say it is cruel to say that, but our best is nothing compared to the Father's least. They would call it cruel because that is not a fair assessment, but how could we ever think that we are on the same level plain as the highest God? Why would you ever think you were capable of being as great as God? You must have lost your mind or what a fool you must be to think you could come close to the Father's goodness! In this false identity and falling state, they would be right, but in our true state, once we have denounced and rejected this false identity, once we grab a hold of our true identity in Christ Jesus, we would see that we are like the Father in every way possible, we just don't know it.

We live in a state of fear, confusion and false identity constantly. We have men who want to be women and women who want to be men; boys who want to be girls and so on. We are not living or walking in truth. Instead, we are making one bad choice after another because we are confused and have been for such a long time, that we think we are enlightened, when we are steeped in darkness; this darkness has falsely covered the true light in us. We have been placed under a bushel when we should have been put on a lamp stand on top of a hill, so all the world could see the glorious light in us from our Father in heaven, ignited and burning because of Christ

Jesus. We are afraid of light. We have turned down our light so we can fit in, be liked or, worse, look like the darkness of the world.

Light will always cast out darkness. There is no darkness so great that light cannot, and will not, cast it out. We are living in the shadows of what we should be. We are skating the edges of how to be because we are walking in a false reflection of light.

Chapter 7
FALSE REFLECTIONS

This false reflection has distorted our view of who we are, so we act in and out of this distortion. We are not darkness, but we accepted it to be true, so it becomes a form of mis-truth: a false truth. We are living as a stranger in our own skin. We have fallen into a dark pit of false identity and called it true identity. We have been miserable in our pursuit of happiness, because we have been seeking the Lord with the ring (false identity), instead of the Lord of the ring or the One who is Lord of lords and King of kings (true identity).

If you were to stop, pause and consider what I am saying for just one moment, you would realize that even in this dark pit, we still see glimpses of our true identity. We can feel the warmth of our Father's goodness so gently, brushing away the pain in our spirit and caressing our souls: those moments, when we feel hope in our darkest hours. You know that moment, when your faith comes and prompts you to do it today, that very thing that you were so afraid of doing yesterday. You know those moments when you have the courage to do the impossible, in the eyes of people. When they have all but counted you out. In these moments we see glimpses of the Father peering through our false identity, leading us gently into the everlasting light. Victory in the middle of the fight, hope in the bed of darkness; we see our God-given nature of love, peace, power and a sound mind coming to the surface. We become, in those moments, who we always were: God's children showing the world the light of life that flows through us, as rushing waters down the rapids of the rivers of Life. We become our true selves: sons of God.

If we could just hold still for a moment, we can hear the still small loving voice of our Father calling us to come home, where He has prepared a place for us at the table of redemption, set with mercy and covered by His grace. If we could just remain fearless for a second longer, we would feel the courage of hope and faith swell up in us from a place that is so deep, so pure, that we would be amazed at who we are in Christ Jesus. But we are not "still" long enough; we are loud, fearful, gong-clamoring about this world, shouting in pain and calling sin good and dark light. We are a lost nation in a valley of confusion, surrounded by people who are not remotely close to knowing themselves.

In the valley of death is where we choose to lay our head, build our homes and raise our children. If we could just look up on the hill, we would see that there are mountain tops where the air is clean and the faith is real. We would see that there is where our help comes from; it comes from on high. We would know our true identity; we would have real peace and get embraced by such a cloud of witnesses, who knows our name and can tell us how to live in and out of our God-given identity. The difference is, we have fallen hook, line and sinker for the lies, deception and false identity of this world. We have become children of the devil by fear. We have bought the false identity and called it true. We have been deceived; we have been tricked and so we suffer.

Why must we suffer? If God is love and so good, why do we suffer so much? We suffer because we refuse to turn from the wicked ways of our false identity. We embraced the lies, instead of rejecting them, and we hold them close as if they were able to give us anything but shame. We cling to them, rather than turn from them. We wear them with false pride, because we think it is who we are.

We suffer because we refuse to let go of our false gods, fake friends and family and seek truth. If we seek the truth of our Father in heaven, and our real family of faith, our suffering would eventually come to an end. We would find peace, joy, faith and love, where pain and suffering used to reside. It is up to us to get up from this place and go to where our Father is calling us.

It is time to go home, to move into a greater place by leaving our false identities behind us. You can have it, if you would just come home. You don't have to die where you were born. You don't have to stay in the pit, you can reach the mountain top, and you can crawl out of the pits of sin and shame. You do not need to be here tomorrow; you can leave and become all that He created you to be. You can walk in faith and trust in the Lord and His love for you. It will take courage and strength to do it. You will have to wash away the old man and put on the new man; the truth of who you are. It will be painful in the beginning, doubt will seek to hold you back and take you captive, as it has so many times before. The devil will rush you with false advertising and fake news of what you would be leaving behind; resist him and he will run from you. Push through, drawing closer to your heavenly Father and He will move closer to you. He calls you by name; He knows you and all the things you did when you were lost, yet He loves you. Will you come home?

How do you regain your identity when it has been stolen? In a world of identity theft, one of the first things you must do is cancel all your credit cards, change passwords and notify your bank that your identity has been stolen. You do this so when the imposter shows up acting like you, they cannot take what is yours. God is telling us to do the same thing; the devil is a thief and he has come as an angel of light, but in reality he is and forever will be the father of lies. How do we change our spiritual password? We use our prayer language; speaking in tongues when we pray. We spend more time listening to the voice of the Father. We don't get confused with all the other voices in the atmosphere.

Lastly, we have to know His ways; we read books and, most importantly, we study the Scriptures to know His character.

The FBI task force that works in the counterfeit bill arena, as part of their training, spend hours studying the authentic US currency, so when they see a fake one, it glows like a red hot piece of coal. They don't spend one second examining the fakes. All of their time is with the authentic; the real. We must do the same when it comes to our heavenly Father; don't give the devil one moment of your time. Spend your time with the Father, so when the devil does come knocking, and he will, his lies will glow like red hot coals and there will be no question as to who he is and what he is about.

Identity Is What Drives Us

Our identity is what gives us direction, background and support to do what God has called us to do. Let me tell you a story about a man who, since he could remember, was told that he was accepted, strong and had something to give to society. His parents edified him, built him up and let him know that he came from a long line of great men and women. What the well-meaning parents did not know was that their son did not identify with them or those words. How do you think the young man turned out? Was the words of his parents enough to shape him into a productive, positive member of society or did his identity win out? These are questions that we have to ask, if we want to get to the root of the identity crisis in the world. The answer is, the son's identity won out; the son did well in sports and academics, until his sophomore year in high school when he took his own life. The suicide note he left his parents read something like this:

> *I know this may hurt you, but I can no longer live this lie anymore. I am not a good person and I am not great. I am a fake and the pressure to be what you want me to be is far too great a burden.*
> *Signed, your son.*

The parents never asked him who he thought he was; they only told him who he was in their eyes. Were the parents wrong for encouraging their son, and telling him the history of how great a family he descended from? I believe they did the right thing. The one thing that every good parent should ask their children is this: "Who do you say you are?" Ask them this question as soon as they can form a whole sentence. Don't wait for the pre-teen years. Why is this important? As they grow, you can help shape them into who they are supposed to be, correct misconceptions and give them purpose. I wish I did this with my children. I have great kids, but they don't know how great they are, because I didn't ask them how they saw themselves or myself. I assumed they knew. The worst approach to parenting is assuming they know. We must be like our Creator, our example and Savior of our souls, Jesus, and ask questions.

Our heavenly Father is always asking us who we say He is to us. He ask us this, by asking us to trust Him in faith: your faith will heal you. If we walk in faith and ask for healing and do not doubt, we are saying He is a Healer. If we step out in faith, when it comes to provision and do not doubt, we are saying He is our Provider. God is always asking us who we say that He is to us. God is everything good, faithful and true, but we don't give Him that position in our times of trouble because our identity is twisted. We often think something is wrong with us. Who are we to ask the God of the universe for something so small as direction in a job, a home, what car to buy or whom we should marry? Why would He care? Why would He answer the questions we ask ourselves? Because we have a false identity of Him and of us, why not just ask the Father? Why do we refuse to trust God in those areas? We are made in His image and likeness; we should identify with Him, since we are made like Him and from Him. We can do what He does in heaven on earth, but we don't because we don't identify with Him. We don't have faith in the fact that we are little gods on the earth. We don't trust Him to do what He said. We are in crisis and the only way out is to let Him call us to our purpose, through us acting in and on faith.

We walk in faith only in the areas where we trust God. No trust, no faith. We don't ask for help from a six year old, when we know the child is not capable of helping us or we don't trust the child to help us. Faith is the substance of things hoped for and the evidence of things not seen (See Hebrews 11:1). So, what does that mean? Here is an illustration: you go to a restaurant and you see this dish on the menu. You read the description or see the picture, whichever, and you decide you want to order that dish. You anticipate that the dish is going to be good or, at least, tasty. You place your order with the waiter, and you continue in preparation for this dish. Once the dish arrives, it is good, actually, better than you hoped. Now let us fast-forward to a year later and you are out with some friends at this same restaurant and they ask you about that same dish. You tell them your experience; you tell them how it was better than you expected. They order the dish and, yes, it was better than advertised for them as well. The dish has built trust; the restaurant has built trust and the chefs have built trust. You and your friends will have no issue testifying in a court of law about how good that dish is; you may even suggest to the jury that they try it for themselves. This is what God is asking us to do: taste and see that He is good but, first, we must trust Him in something so He can show us that He is good.

You had some faith in the restaurant; you went there and gave them your money, time and attention. You ate the food and loved it. This is faith, at its best. You envisioned an experience at this particular place; you stepped out in faith and went to the place; you stepped out deeper and ordered off the menu from a place you don't know, from people you can't see, with an expectation that the food is going to be good. This all takes faith; this all requires trust.

God is asking us to do the same thing: tell others about how good He is and has been to us. Let our experience with Him shape our identity in ourselves and others. God will never have an identity crisis. He will never say, "I don't know who I am today" or "I don't feel quite like being Myself, so let Me be someone else today." That is never going to happen. God knows who

He is and what He is about. The question remains, do you? Who are you? What are you about?

We drive cars with badges from Chevy, Lexus, Cadillac, Mercedes Benz, Rolls-Royce, etc. The value comes from the purchaser; the name came from the creator. A name is part of an identity, but it is not the identity. Identity is built on three things: name, experience and expression or purpose. What you call a thing, is its name. The experience you expect from what you called it and how the thing is expressing itself in its intended environment, is its nature. Going back to the cars, the creator had in mind what type of car it would be, how it would perform, its expression and how the customer would experience that performance.

Based on the intended experience the purchaser was going to have, the creator built in that experience. They had a vision of how the buyer would expect to express those qualities, so they built in those as well. When a car does not live up to the purpose or its name, and the buyer is not able to express or draw out those experiences in the vehicle, the manufacturer will often recall that car. They are recalling the car because it is not living up to its original design; it is not walking in the identity of its creator.

Our recall is what religious folks would say is a call to the faith or they found Jesus, as if He was lost. The thought is funny. God sent Jesus to do a massive recall on all humanity, with the death, burial and resurrection of His only begotten Son. Jesus is offering to fix the defects in us, all by asking us to be remanufactured (born again). This process is accepting Jesus as our Lord and Savior, confessing our sins, acceptance of His gift and being baptized in the Word, water and allowing the Holy Spirit to come into us and fill us, with the evidence of speaking in tongues. This spiritual recall is to fix our broken identity and straighten out our crooked ways. His ways now become our ways and His strength replaces our brokenness.

Our Father God wants to give us an upgrade, similar to when a car manufacturer sends out a recall. They discovered an issue and want to repair it, so the buyer can have the experience they expect from the name and express that joy to others.

Chapter 8
WHO TOLD YOU THAT YOU WERE NAKED?

*W*ho told you that you were naked? Did you eat from the tree of knowledge which I forbade you not to eat? (See Genesis 3:11). These questions were asked of Adam in the Garden of Eden. Because he was no longer secure in his identity, he

137

quickly placed the blame on his wife and God. "This woman you gave me, she gave me to eat and I did it" (See Genesis 3:12). As you can tell, the lack of identity came from disobedience. Listen to this in Genesis 2:16-17:

> *And the Lord God commanded the man, saying, "Of every tree of the garden you may freely eat; but of the tree of the knowledge of good and evil you shall not eat, for in the day that you eat of it you shall surely die."*

Now the question most would ask is: "If You did not want me to eat it, why would You put it there in the first place?" That is a question I will answer quickly. He put it there so we would have a choice to obey or disobey. If there were no options, we would obey by default. If there is no choice, there is no real obedience. I believe God put the tree there for them to choose, and He was careful to warn Adam of the consequences, if they choose this over that. He gave man choice; He told him the consequences of the choice. Now back to the subject matter of the tree of the knowledge of good and evil. Prior to the fall, man only knew God and His sovereign will; His orders and His reign. Adam and Eve only had a God-identity prior to being disobedient. They only knew who they were in the eyes of the Father. Fast forward to after they had eaten the fruit of the tree of the knowledge of good and evil; they became aware of themselves and their nakedness and were ashamed, so they hid from God. It is safe to say, they lost their identity at that moment.

Knowledge is good, if it is in the right context. Knowledge of God is good. When God made humans, they were good. He made us in His image. He gave us our identity. He called us good. When we fell and were removed from the Garden, we took on the identity of the prince of darkness; the devil. Here is where the struggle for identity started. The identity issue has become an epidemic in the world with, for example, men who say they are women; women who say they are men; women who want to do everything a man should do, and men who let them because they refuse to stand in their position as the head of the family, that is, the responsible party. I am going to be transparent here; I was just like that. I let my wife do what I should have done, not because I could not, but because I chose me over we. I chose myself over God's order. Self was my focus and God was an afterthought, if a thought. I am not telling you this because it sounds good. I am sharing this because I have been through it. I am a survivor of my ego; my marriage survived my ego; my family survived my ego. Why? It was not because of me; I was a walking disaster. It was because my Father in heaven let it be so. It was His will, not mine.

I was asking for a rope out of my pit, but when the rope came, I often cut it up and say that it was not good enough. I self-sabotaged my present and my future, all because I did not know who I was. Thank you, Father, for not giving up on me. Thank You for giving me grace when I was hell-bent on destroying myself, with myself. I struggle at times, even today, with my dead self. I know countless others who have similar daily, moment by moment struggles as well.

What is the answer? When does it end? Some would say it is because we are in the last days and that is true, but does that release us from being who our Father called us to be because the world is going down? No, it does not. In fact, it should push us closer to God and give us more compassion for the lost in the world. Instead, good people refuse to do good, so evil reigns.

When did it become okay to make up the truth and not call it what it really is: a lie. A lie is something that is untrue, with the intent to deceive the hearer. We cannot allow this delusional state of affairs to continue and not do something about it. Well, yes we can, because we have lost our identity.

Until we recognize, reconnect and reconcile in ourselves that we are unique and valuable as we are, and that God made us with and for purpose, we will continue to have identity issues.

Man did not make you, so man cannot provide you with your true identity. Man can give you false ones but only the Father can give you your real identity. Take a look at this:

> *Exodus 3:14*
> *And God said to Moses, "I AM WHO I AM." And He said, "Thus you shall say to the children of Israel, 'I AM has sent me to you.'"*

God is talking to Moses and giving him instructions of what to tell the Pharaoh of Egypt and the people of Israel. He was telling Moses who He was, meaning God. God said, "I AM" has sent you. God gives everything identity because He is the beginning and the end; the first and the last.

> *Revelation 22:13*
>
> *I am the Alpha and the Omega, the Beginning and the End, the First and the Last.*

You can do nothing without God. He created us to be like Him and He gave us dominion over all His creation.

> *Genesis 1:26*
>
> *Then God said, "Let Us make man in Our image, according to Our likeness; let them have dominion over the fish of the sea, over the birds of the air, and over the cattle, over all the earth and over every creeping thing that creeps on the earth."*

God made us all in His image, with His likeness. In His image: we are a reflection of Him; in His likeness: our nature is similar to His. God is a Spirit; we are a spirit. God is love; we have a need to love and be loved. From the beginning of time, God gave us our identity. He said we are like Him.

> *Jeremiah 1:5*
> *Before I formed you in the womb I knew you; before you were born I sanctified you; I ordained you a prophet to the nations.*

In the above text, God is talking to Jeremiah, but the same can be said about us. He knew us before we came into the womb. He called us to a purpose before we were ever born.

There is no reason for us to have an identity crisis, but we do. We are in crisis because we believed the lie and falsely loved the lie. Satan told Eve that if she ate the forbidden fruit, she would be like God. She was already like God; we are made in His image and likeness. We are good, not good without Him, only good with Him. We are not invisible to God; we are not alone either. Do not allow your lack of identity to keep you from moving forward in finding out who you are in God's grand design. The answer is in Christ; your identity can be found in Him. You will never find your identity in a job, a bottle, a person or in a drug. You will only find your true identity in Christ Jesus, which leads you to the Father where the real you resides. Don't search out the counterfeit, when you can have the real thing in the Father, through a personal relationship with the Father.

Chapter 9
LETTER FROM OUR HEAVENLY FATHER

I f your life is in turmoil, check your identity: who did I say you were? Why has your countenance fallen? If you had done well, would you not have been accepted? Do you know the only reason you are still breathing is because I see more in you? You are alive because I am giving you time to discover my Son, Jesus, and the hidden treasures I hid within you, for the betterment of the world and yourself. I am waiting for you to turn and come home.

You are not a mistake. Your life is Mine and how you are living is by your choice or lack thereof. I sent my Son, Jesus, to you, so you could have life and have it more abundantly. You are not living your best life. You are living in the valley of death, when I placed you on mountain tops with green pastures.

You have given up on life because you are afraid to fail. Let me give you some history to the mystery of your life. Before your mother and father were formed in their parents womb, I knew you. You are, because I ordained you to be. Nothing will prevent you from being your best, except you. All the power in heaven and hell that I gave to Jesus, He left it with you. Why are you not using the power?

I hear your prayers, but some things I left in your scope of control. What you do, how you do and when you do is all in your scope. When you pray, you are asking Me to do it, I will not move past your free will. You must use your free will to choose. I will speak to you and give you instructions, but you have to act on those instructions.

If you don't move forward, you leave My hands tied. If you want more, you must lose more or give more. Lose more of what you think it should be, so you can gain more of what I am sharing with you. Think of it this way: if you are a vessel that can hold five gallons, and you pour out a half gallon, you only have the capacity for a half gallon. You are too full of you to receive any of Me. So pour you out, so I can fill you with Me. Once you allow yourself to be poured out, and Me to fill you, you will soon realize that I am good for you and to you.

Your fear of not knowing has kept you from growing. Not knowing what is next or how it is going to happen has caused you to remain stagnant, not growing, complaining about this and that, and feeling hopeless. You are not hopeless, but you feel that way because you have lost the gratitude and love for what is. Instead, you seek after false gods, false hope, false identity and fill yourself with their ways and refuse Mine. What are these false gods? Let me tell you: selfishness, fornication, greed, lust, murder, drunkenness, adultery, doubt, fear, discontentment, hate, religion, judgment of others and disobedience. These are the gods you follow in various areas of your life. I know you want Me, but the question is, do you want Me more than you want you? Your fear is holding you captive. Your fear of not being like Me is what drove you to disobey Me in the garden. You felt like I was keeping something from you that was good for you, when in reality, I was keeping you from destroying yourself. You were made in My image and My likeness from the beginning, but you allowed an outsider to tell you something different, something other than what I have shown you about Me.

You chose to follow the voice of a stranger and not the voice of a loving Father who has always provided for you. You thought that his way was better than the way I had laid out for you. You broke My heart by being disobedient, so I had to curse the ground for you. I made you good, but you did wrong, so the earth has to suffer for you, since you wanted to follow the false teacher, Satan, and listen to all his lies. When you followed him, you lost access to paradise and you lost access to Me. This is why I sent my only begotten Son. I sent Him to restore you back to Me, to give you access to My full and complete love.

I did not bring you religion, I brought you relationship. I did not bring you rules and regulations, I gave you boundaries with liberty. All that you are suffering is not because I did not love you. You are suffering because you would not follow the path I placed in front of you. You are suffering because you don't know who you are and refuse to believe who I AM. Your suffering is because you forgot your true self and My promise to never leave you or forsake you. You bought a lie, lived a lie and now you are suffering in pain for that lie. What is the lie: the way you are now is not worthy of love; you are nothing special; you will always be what you have always been. That is the lie; who told you that? I know I did not tell you anything like that. I told you, through My prophets and the Scriptures, that you are loved. Why do you think I gave you My Son? I gave you Jesus because I love you.

I will never go beyond your free will. I will never make you do anything. I can, but I won't. The devil can't make you do anything, but that doesn't prevent him from trying. So, My child, here is the answer to all the questions that you may have. Obey My voice, and all things will work out for your good. Love My voice, get to know My voice, seek a deep relationship with Me and My voice, so I can direct your path.

I am sorry you have been led astray by wolves in sheep's clothing. That was not My intention or plan for you. You made a choice and that choice came with consequences, and pain is a result of that choice. You have an opportunity to move beyond that way of life and move into a better way.

You will have pain, but it won't be for nothing. It will help you to produce more fruit. You will have setbacks, so you can grow bigger and stronger. I have plans for you and that is, and will always be, to give you a hope and a future. Please hear Me, and accept My gift: My only begotten Son as a ransom for your disobedience, so you can come back home.

I miss you, My child. I have sent preachers, teachers and prophets to you. I sent them to tell you about My love for you. They failed because they let the spotlight shining on them dim the light that was in them. This is why I sent My Son, Jesus. I knew He would only do and say what I do and say. He is the way, the truth, and the life. No one can come to Me, except through Him. Accept My gift of reconciliation; I want you home. Bring your brothers and sisters when you come. I miss all of you and love all of you. I know you may feel guilty for not listening: confess those sins to one another, repent and I am quick to forgive you. Will you come home? I will leave the light on.

Love
God, your Father

Chapter 10
WE ARE NOT WHO WE THINK WE ARE. WE ARE MORE, MUCH MORE

We must understand this fact, if we want to walk in continuous victory. We must lay this to rest: we are not who we think we are, we are who God says we are. His Word must always supersede our own and surely the words of others. His

Word must be the first and last word. What we see, is not true; it is an illusion. What we think is not real until we speak it into the atmosphere.

If we don't want to live a life of "me"-filled mistakes, laced with selfish heartaches and capped with the pain of our ego, then we must let God be God; we must yield to Him in all things, especially when it comes to our identity. We are not a mistake; we are not sin-filled when we rest in the precious gift of Christ. We are a new creation in Christ Jesus, so we must put on our new identity every moment of the day.

We cannot allow our past errors, sins and selfish heart to keep us captive to that old person. If we have accepted Jesus as our Lord and Savior, then it is settled: we are a new creation, a new being with a new identity. If we are new, then we must act like we know who we are new and to whom we belong. Our identity is no longer in our biological family, jobs, careers or the work of our hands.

Genesis 15:1
After these things the word of the Lord came to Abram in a vision, saying, "Do not be afraid, Abram. I am your shield, your exceedingly great reward."

Life is full of doubt, fear and distrust, but that is not a reason to stop living. People will be people; they will disappoint and hurt you, and break your trust. That is why we need to trust in our Creator, our Manufacturer: God. As the above verse states, God wants to be our shield, actually, He says He is our shield. He is our protection from the darkness of the world.

When God says, "I AM that I AM," He is saying several things in one statement. He is a person, of sorts, and a person is someone who has personality, dreams, ideas and visions. He is also stating that He is the definition of I AM. He was and always has been, not made, shaped or created; He just is. He is also telling us that He is real, not something out there, but right here, right now. He said: tell them that I AM has sent you.

What a powerful verse, "I AM has sent you." I want to tell you that I AM has sent you into the world to set His people free. He has loaded you up with gifts, talents, skills and a passion for a portion of the world. This portion is what drives you; it is that fire that burns in you, when you see it not being taken care of. It is that compassion you feel when you see someone being mistreated or misused or their gift going underutilized. It is what angers you and compels you to act. If you have not experienced that, sad to say, you have not lived; you have only existed. Life without passion for life is not a life. Christ came that we would have life and have it more abundantly. Passion is a part of that abundant life. Get passionate about something, so you do something and make something better for yourself and others.

You are not living, if you don't have anything that drives you to make something better. You are the living dead, if you have not found at least one thing that brings a smile to your face and joy to your heart, when you help someone be better in some area of life. Contrary to popular belief, you need someone to be your best self. You will never be your best self, if you stay isolated with a lone-wolf mentality and think you are self-made. We are created to share and rely on each other. I cannot watch my own back, and neither can you. We need one another to help shape us into our best selves.

You are more than you have experienced up to this point. You have more to give than you have given, and more to learn than you have learned up to this point. Age don't matter. You can be 109+ and still be going strong, and you would still have more to learn, more to give and more to experience. If you have breath, you have more to do.

> *Genesis 17:1*
>
> *When Abram was ninety-nine years old, the Lord appeared to Abram and said to him, "I am Almighty God; walk before Me and be blameless."*

God appeared to Abram when he was ninety-nine years old, and told him that He is God Almighty and he should walk blameless before Him. He did not tell Abram that he was up in age and He would understand if he could not do what was being asked of him. That is not what God said. God told Abram who He is and gave Abram instructions.

> *Genesis 26:24*
>
> *And the Lord appeared to him the same night and said, "I am the God of your father Abraham; do not fear, for I am with you. I will bless you and multiply your descendants for My servant Abraham's sake."*

God is telling us the same thing: not to be afraid to trust Him and He will bless us.

Genesis 28:15

Behold, I am with you and will keep you wherever you go, and will bring you back to this land; for I will not leave you until I have done what I have spoken to you.

When our Father sent you to the planet, He told you what you were supposed to do. He put it in you and was going to use the pain, trials and tribulations of life to dig it out of you. His will is that we fulfill what He has spoken to us. We have to do it because He will not do it for us. We must move towards it. He put it in our path, not in our hands.

Genesis 31:13

I am the God of Bethel, where you anointed the pillar and where you made a vow to Me. Now arise, get out of this land, and return to the land of your family.

Genesis 35:11

Also God said to him: "I am God Almighty. Be fruitful and multiply; a nation and a company of nations shall proceed from you, and kings shall come from your body."

Genesis 46:3

So He said, "I am God, the God of your father; do not fear to go down to Egypt, for I will make of you a great nation there."

Exodus 3:14

And God said to Moses, "I AM WHO I AM." And He said, "Thus you shall say to the children of Israel, 'I AM has sent me to you.'"

Exodus 4:10

Then Moses said to the Lord, "O my Lord, I am not eloquent, neither before nor since You have spoken to Your servant;

> *but I am slow of speech and slow of tongue."*

I am calling you by faith. If you have made it this far in this book, you have had an encounter with our Heavenly Father. Do me a favor and don't be like Moses and make excuses as to why you can't do what the Creator designed, purposed and planted you on the earth to do. If He called you to it, He has already equipped you to do it.

> *Exodus 6:2-3*
>
> *And God spoke to Moses and said to him: "I am the Lord. I appeared to Abraham, to Isaac, and to Jacob, as God Almighty, but by My name Lord I was not known to them."*

God knows your name; He knows your identity. Do you know His? God is watching and waiting for His children, which He made joint-heirs with His Son, Jesus, to take their place in the kingdom of heaven on earth. Are you confused about who you are, so you settle for what they call you? They call you fear, so you respond afraid. They call you doubt, so you respond with unsureness in your life. God called you mighty, wonderful and more than a conquer, so why not respond to those names?

> *Exodus 6:6-8*
>
> *Therefore say to the children of Israel: 'I am the Lord; I will bring you out from under the burdens of the Egyptians, I will rescue you from their bondage, and I will redeem you with an outstretched arm and with great judgments. I will take you as My people, and I will be your God. Then you shall know that I am the Lord your God who brings you out from under the burdens of the Egyptians. And I will bring you into the land which I swore to give to Abraham, Isaac, and Jacob; and I will give it to you as a heritage: I am the Lord.*

God made us a promise: no matter where we go, He will be with us. No matter what we face, He will be alongside us. No matter what we need, He will provide it, according to His richness and glory. We are the reason that we suffer, not Him. We must accept and hold on to the promise. I AM is with us and nothing can stand against us, since I AM is on and by our side.

Exodus 7:17

Thus says the Lord: "By this you shall know that I am the Lord. Behold, I will strike the waters which are in the river with the rod that is in my hand, and they shall be turned to blood."

Exodus 8:22

And in that day I will set apart the land of Goshen, in which My people dwell, that no swarms of flies shall be there, in order that you may know that I am the Lord in the midst of the land.

Exodus 10:2

And that you may tell in the hearing of your son and your son's son the mighty things I have done in Egypt, and My signs which I have done among them, that you may know that I am the Lord.

Chapter 11
STOP TRYING TO BE WHAT THEY WANT AND START TO BE WHAT HE WANTS

The Bible is the inspired Word of God, and it is used for the building, teaching and training of the saints. It is not the only Word of God. God is a right here and now God. He is talking to you at this very moment, telling you something He needs you to do. Do not think the only way God speaks is from the Bible; that is His Word, but it is not all He has to say. God is never sleeping or is ever surprised by us, His creation; His children. Where you are now, God saw you heading that way before you were aware of where you were going.

Stop trying to be what they want, and start to be what He wants. You have a purpose. You came filled with a mission, and your mouth and feet are your weapons of warfare, so guard them, know them and use them to be what God called you to be. Do not think you can't do it, when God said you can. If God gave it to you, He will give you what you need to maintain and grow it.

God is an investor, and He invested the life of His Son, Jesus, in you. God is looking for a return on that investment. He knows that if you don't know who you are, you will never be able to give Him a return. I am here to tell you that you are more than you think, and you can do more than you have done up to this point. You are more than they (the world) think, not in the way of boasting or pride, but more in the way of purpose, passion and gifts that have yet to be poured out. Pour out what you have been given, and wait for the harvest to come back to you.

3-Jay found his voice, but he had to let go of who he thought he was and trust the gift. He also had to be willing to change his perspective. The same is true for us as well. We have to trust the gift, which is Jesus Christ, and move our perspective from religion to relationship. We are no different when it comes to identity crisis; we are not immune to it either. The advantage that we have is that we can move ahead with the knowledge of this one truth: no matter where we are in life, no matter the age or stage, our Father is standing by waiting for us to come home, with a prepared feast. Often the crisis is in our minds and the battle is fought and won in our minds. To discover your true identity in the middle of a crisis we have to change our mind. Repent from your old self; repent means to turn away from. Repent and move towards the Father. Let go of what you think, replace it with this one truth: God loves you, and will never leave you nor forsake you. He is always there waiting to share His love with you. Will you leave the pit of confusion and grab hold of the Lord's hand?

God knows your heart; do you know His? God wants you to live by faith, not by fear and definitely not by sight. Don't make an eternal choice based on the shifting sands of the temporal. You are not a failure; you are not a waste of space and you are not worthless. God is calling you by the names He gave you: victorious, faithful, courageous, mighty, strong sons and daughters through Christ Jesus. God did not give you the names they called you when you failed, messed up or made a mistake.

Who are you, is the question. The answer must always be: I am who I AM says that I am.

Know yourself and be true to that self.

Until next time...

I AM SAYS THE FOLLOWING

Genesis 15:1: After these things the word of the Lord came to Abram in a vision, saying, "Do not be afraid, Abram. I am your shield, your exceedingly great reward."

Genesis 15:7: Then He said to him, "I am the Lord, who brought you out of Ur of the Chaldeans, to give you this land to inherit it."

Genesis 17:1: When Abram was ninety-nine years old the LORD appeared to Abram and said to him, "I am God Almighty; walk before me, and be blameless."

Genesis 18:17: And the Lord said, "Shall I hide from Abraham what I am doing."

Note: Our Father does keep things from us, when He is about to bless us with something major.

Genesis 28:13: And behold, the Lord stood above it and said: "I am the Lord God of Abraham your father and the God of Isaac; the land on which you lie I will give to you and your descendants."

Exodus 6:2: And God spoke to Moses and said to him: "I am the Lord."

Exodus 6:6: Therefore say to the children of Israel: 'I am the Lord; I will bring you out from under the burdens of the Egyptians, I will rescue you from their bondage, and I will redeem you with an outstretched arm and with great judgments.'

Exodus 6:7: I will take you as My people, and I will be your God. Then you shall know that I am the Lord your God who brings you out from under the burdens of the Egyptians.

Exodus 6:8: And I will bring you into the land which I swore to give to Abraham, Isaac, and Jacob; and I will give it to you as a heritage: I am the Lord.

Exodus 6:29: That the Lord spoke to Moses, saying, "I am the Lord. Speak to Pharaoh king of Egypt all that I say to you."

Exodus 7:5: And the Egyptians shall know that I am the Lord, when I stretch out My hand on Egypt and bring out the children of Israel from among them.

Exodus 7:17: Thus says the Lord: "By this you shall know that I am the Lord. Behold, I will strike the waters which are in the river with the rod that is in my hand, and they shall be turned to blood."

Exodus 8:22: And in that day I will set apart the land of Goshen, in which My people dwell, that no swarms of flies shall be there, in order that you may know that I am the Lord in the midst of the land.

Exodus 10:2: And that you may tell in the hearing of your son and your son's son the mighty things I have done in Egypt, and My signs which I have done among them, that you may know that I am the Lord.

Exodus 12:12: For I will pass through the land of Egypt on that night, and will strike all the firstborn in the land of Egypt, both man and beast; and against all the gods of Egypt I will execute judgment: I am the Lord.

Exodus 14:4: "Then I will harden Pharaoh's heart, so that he will pursue them; and I will gain honor over Pharaoh and over all his army, that the Egyptians may know that I am the Lord." And they did so.

Exodus 14:18: Then the Egyptians shall know that I am the Lord, when I have gained honor for Myself over Pharaoh, his chariots, and his horsemen.

Exodus 15:26: And said, "If you diligently heed the voice of the Lord your God and do what is right in His sight, give ear to His commandments and keep all His statutes, I will put none of the diseases on you which I have brought on the Egyptians. For I am the Lord who heals you."

Exodus 16:12: "I have heard the complaints of the children of Israel. Speak to them, saying, 'At twilight you shall eat meat, and in the morning you shall be filled with bread. And you shall know that I am the Lord your God.'"

Exodus 20:2: I am the Lord your God, who brought you out of the land of Egypt, out of the house of bondage.

Exodus 29:46: And they shall know that I am the Lord their God, who brought them up out of the land of Egypt, that I may dwell among them. I am the Lord their God.

Leviticus 11:44: For I am the Lord your God. You shall therefore consecrate yourselves, and you shall be holy; for I am holy. Neither shall you defile yourselves with any creeping thing that creeps on the earth.

Leviticus 11:45: For I am the Lord who brings you up out of the land of Egypt, to be your God. You shall therefore be holy, for I am holy.

Leviticus 18:2: Speak to the children of Israel, and say to them: 'I am the Lord your God.'

Leviticus 18:4: You shall observe My judgments and keep My ordinances, to walk in them: I am the Lord your God.

Leviticus 18:5: You shall therefore keep My statutes and My judgments, which if a man does, he shall live by them: I am the Lord.

Leviticus 18:6: None of you shall approach anyone who is near of kin to him, to uncover his nakedness: I am the Lord.

Leviticus 18:21: And you shall not let any of your descendants pass through the fire to Molech, nor shall you profane the name of your God: I am the Lord.

Leviticus 18:30: 'Therefore you shall keep My ordinance, so that you do not commit any of these abominable customs which were committed before you, and that you do not defile yourselves by them: I am the Lord your God.'

Leviticus 19:3: Every one of you shall revere his mother and his father, and keep My Sabbaths: I am the Lord your God.

Leviticus 19:4: Do not turn to idols, nor make for yourselves molded gods: I am the Lord your God.

Leviticus 19:10: And you shall not glean your vineyard, nor shall you gather every grape of your vineyard; you shall leave them for the poor and the stranger: I am the Lord your God.

Leviticus 19:12: And you shall not swear by My name falsely, nor shall you profane the name of your God: I am the Lord.

Leviticus 19:14: You shall not curse the deaf, nor put a stumbling block before the blind, but shall fear your God: I am the Lord.

Leviticus 19:16: You shall not go about as a talebearer among your people; nor shall you take a stand against the life of your neighbor: I am the Lord.

Leviticus 19:18: You shall not take vengeance, nor bear any grudge against the children of your people, but you shall love your neighbor as yourself: I am the Lord.

Leviticus 19:25: And in the fifth year you may eat its fruit, that it may yield to you its increase: I am the Lord your God.

Leviticus 19:28: You shall not make any cuttings in your flesh for the dead, nor tattoo any marks on you: I am the Lord.

Leviticus 19:30: You shall keep My Sabbaths and reverence My sanctuary: I am the Lord.

Leviticus 19:31: Give no regard to mediums and familiar spirits; do not seek after them, to be defiled by them: I am the Lord your God.

Leviticus 19:32: You shall rise before the gray headed and honor the presence of an old man, and fear your God: I am the Lord.

Leviticus 19:34: The stranger who dwells among you shall be to you as one born among you, and you shall love him as yourself; for you were strangers in the land of Egypt: I am the Lord your God.

Leviticus 19:36: You shall have honest scales, honest weights, an honest ephah, and an honest hin: I am the Lord your God, who brought you out of the land of Egypt.

Leviticus 19:37: Therefore you shall observe all My statutes and all My judgments, and perform them: I am the Lord.

Leviticus 20:7: Consecrate yourselves therefore, and be holy, for I am the Lord your God.

Leviticus 20:8: And you shall keep My statutes, and perform them: I am the Lord who sanctifies you.

Leviticus 20:24: But I have said to you, "You shall inherit their land, and I will give it to you to possess, a land flowing with milk and honey." I am the Lord your God, who has separated you from the peoples.

Leviticus 21:12: Nor shall he go out of the sanctuary, nor profane the sanctuary of his God; for the consecration of the anointing oil of his God is upon him: I am the Lord.

Leviticus 21:15: Nor shall he profane his posterity among his people, for I the Lord sanctify him.

Leviticus 21:23: Only he shall not go near the veil or approach the altar, because he has a defect, lest he profane My sanctuaries; for I the Lord sanctify them.

Leviticus 22:2: Speak to Aaron and his sons, that they separate themselves from the holy things of the children of Israel, and that they do not profane My holy name by what they dedicate to Me: I am the Lord.

Leviticus 22:3: Say to them: 'Whoever of all your descendants throughout your generations, who goes near the holy things which the children of Israel dedicate to the Lord, while he has uncleanness upon him, that person shall be cut off from My presence: I am the Lord.'

Leviticus 22:8: Whatever dies naturally or is torn by beasts he shall not eat, to defile himself with it: I am the Lord.

Leviticus 22:9: They shall therefore keep My ordinance, lest they bear sin for it and die thereby, if they profane it: I the Lord sanctify them.

Leviticus 22:16: Or allow them to bear the guilt of trespass when they eat their holy offerings; for I the Lord sanctify them.

Leviticus 22:30: On the same day it shall be eaten; you shall leave none of it until morning: I am the Lord.

Leviticus 22:31: Therefore you shall keep My commandments, and perform them: I am the Lord.

Leviticus 22:32: You shall not profane My holy name, but I will be hallowed among the children of Israel. I am the Lord who sanctifies you.

Leviticus 22:33: Who brought you out of the land of Egypt, to be your God: I am the Lord.

Leviticus 23:22: 'When you reap the harvest of your land, you shall not wholly reap the corners of your field when you reap, nor shall you gather any gleaning from your harvest. You shall leave them for the poor and for the stranger: I am the Lord your God.'

Leviticus 23:43: That your generations may know that I made the children of Israel dwell in booths when I brought them out of the land of Egypt: I am the Lord your God.

Leviticus 24:22: You shall have the same law for the stranger and for one from your own country; for I am the Lord your God.

Leviticus 25:17: Therefore you shall not oppress one another, but you shall fear your God; for I am the Lord your God.

Leviticus 25:38: I am the Lord your God, who brought you out of the land of Egypt, to give you the land of Canaan and to be your God.

Leviticus 25:55: For the children of Israel are servants to Me; they are My servants whom I brought out of the land of Egypt: I am the Lord your God.

Leviticus 26:1: You shall not make idols for yourselves; neither a carved image nor a sacred pillar shall you rear up for yourselves; nor shall you set up an engraved stone in your land, to bow down to it; for I am the Lord your God.

Leviticus 26:2: You shall keep My Sabbaths and reverence My sanctuary: I am the Lord.

Leviticus 26:13: I am the Lord your God, who brought you out of the land of Egypt, that you should not be their slaves; I have broken the bands of your yoke and made you walk upright.

Leviticus 26:44: Yet for all that, when they are in the land of their enemies, I will not cast them away, nor shall I abhor them, to utterly destroy them and break My covenant with them; for I am the Lord their God.

Leviticus 26:45: But for their sake I will remember the covenant of their ancestors, whom I brought out of the land of Egypt in the sight of the nations, that I might be their God: I am the Lord.

Numbers 3:13: Because all the firstborn are Mine. On the day that I struck all the firstborn in the land of Egypt, I sanctified to Myself all the firstborn in Israel, both man and beast. They shall be Mine: I am the Lord.

Numbers 3:41: And you shall take the Levites for Me—I am the Lord—instead of all the firstborn among the children of Israel, and the livestock of the Levites instead of all the firstborn among the livestock of the children of Israel.

Numbers 3:45: Take the Levites instead of all the firstborn among the children of Israel, and the livestock of the Levites instead of their livestock. The Levites shall be Mine: I am the Lord.

Numbers 10:10: Also in the day of your gladness, in your appointed feasts, and at the beginning of your months, you shall blow the trumpets over your burnt offerings and over the sacrifices of your peace offerings; and they shall be a memorial for you before your God: I am the Lord your God.

Numbers 15:41: I am the Lord your God, who brought you out of the land of Egypt, to be your God: I am the Lord your God.

Deuteronomy 5:6: I am the Lord your God who brought you out of the land of Egypt, out of the house of bondage.

Deuteronomy 29:6: You have not eaten bread, nor have you drunk wine or similar drink, that you may know that I am the Lord your God.

Judges 6:10: Also I said to you, "I am the Lord your God; do not fear the gods of the Amorites, in whose land you dwell." But you have not obeyed My voice.

1 Kings 20:13: Suddenly a prophet approached Ahab king of Israel, saying, "Thus says the Lord: 'Have you seen all this great multitude? Behold, I will deliver it into your hand today, and you shall know that I am the Lord.'"

1 Kings 20:28: Then a man of God came and spoke to the king of Israel, and said, "Thus says the Lord: 'Because the Syrians have said, "The Lord is God of the hills, but He is not God of the valleys," therefore I will deliver all this great multitude into your hand, and you shall know that I am the Lord.'"

Psalms 81:10: I am the Lord your God, who brought you out of the land of Egypt; open your mouth wide, and I will fill it.

Isaiah 42:6: I, the Lord, have called You in righteousness, and will hold Your hand; I will keep You and give You as a covenant to the people, as a light to the Gentiles.

Isaiah 42:8: I am the Lord, that is My name; and My glory I will not give to another, nor My praise to carved images.

Isaiah 43:3: For I am the Lord your God, the Holy One of Israel, your Savior; I gave Egypt for your ransom, Ethiopia and Seba in your place.

Isaiah 43:11: I, even I, am the Lord, and besides Me there is no savior.

Isaiah 43:15: I am the Lord, your Holy One, the Creator of Israel, your King.

Isaiah 44:5: One will say, 'I am the Lord's'; another will call himself by the name of Jacob; another will write with his hand, 'The Lord's,' and name himself by the name of Israel.

Isaiah 44:24: Thus says the Lord, your Redeemer, and He who formed you from the womb: "I am the Lord, who makes all things, who stretches out the heavens all alone, who spreads abroad the earth by Myself."

Isaiah 45:5: I am the Lord, and there is no other; there is no God besides Me. I will gird you, though you have not known Me.

Isaiah 45:6: That they may know from the rising of the sun to its setting that there is none besides Me. I am the Lord, and there is no other.

Isaiah 45:7: I form the light and create darkness, I make peace and create calamity; I, the Lord, do all these things.

Isaiah 45:18: For thus says the Lord, who created the heavens, who is God, who formed the earth and made it, who has established it, who did not create it in vain, who formed it to be inhabited: "I am the Lord, and there is no other."

Isaiah 48:12: Listen to Me, O Jacob, and Israel, My called: I am He, I am the First, I am also the Last.

Isaiah 48:17: Thus says the Lord, your Redeemer, the Holy One of Israel: "I am the Lord your God, who teaches you to profit, who leads you by the way you should go."

Isaiah 49:23: Kings shall be your foster fathers, and their queens your nursing mothers; they shall bow down to you with their faces to the earth, and lick up the dust of your feet. Then you will know that I am the Lord, for they shall not be ashamed who wait for Me.

Isaiah 49:26: I will feed those who oppress you with their own flesh, and they shall be drunk with their own blood as with sweet wine. All flesh shall know that I, the Lord, am your Savior, and your Redeemer, the Mighty One of Jacob.

Isaiah 51:15: But I am the Lord your God, who divided the sea whose waves roared— the Lord of hosts is His name.

Isaiah 60:22: A little one shall become a thousand, and a small one a strong nation. I, the Lord, will hasten it in its time.

Jeremiah 9:24: "But let him who glories glory in this, that he understands and knows Me, that I am the Lord, exercising lovingkindness, judgment, and righteousness in the earth. For in these I delight," says the Lord.

Jeremiah 24:7: Then I will give them a heart to know Me, that I am the Lord; and they shall be My people, and I will be their God, for they shall return to Me with their whole heart.

Jeremiah 32:27: Behold, I am the Lord, the God of all flesh. Is there anything too hard for Me?

Ezekiel 5:13: Thus shall My anger be spent, and I will cause My fury to rest upon them, and I will be avenged; and they shall know that I, the Lord, have spoken it in My zeal, when I have spent My fury upon them.

Ezekiel 5:15: So it shall be a reproach, a taunt, a lesson, and an astonishment to the nations that are all around you, when I execute judgments among you in anger and in fury and in furious rebukes. I, the Lord, have spoken.

Ezekiel 5:17: So I will send against you famine and wild beasts, and they will bereave you. Pestilence and blood shall pass through you, and I will bring the sword against you. I, the Lord, have spoken.

Ezekiel 6:7: The slain shall fall in your midst, and you shall know that I am the Lord.

Ezekiel 6:10: And they shall know that I am the Lord; I have not said in vain that I would bring this calamity upon them.

Ezekiel 6:13: Then you shall know that I am the Lord, when their slain are among their idols all around their altars, on every high hill, on all the mountaintops, under every green tree, and under every thick oak, wherever they offered sweet incense to all their idols.

Ezekiel 6:14: So I will stretch out My hand against them and make the land desolate, yes, more desolate than the wilderness toward Diblah, in all their dwelling places. Then they shall know that I am the Lord.

Ezekiel 7:4: My eye will not spare you, nor will I have pity; but I will repay your ways, and your abominations will be in your midst; then you shall know that I am the Lord!

Ezekiel 7:9: My eye will not spare, nor will I have pity; I will repay you according to your ways, and your abominations will be in your midst. Then you shall know that I am the Lord who strikes.

Ezekiel 7:27: The king will mourn, the prince will be clothed with desolation, and the hands of the common people will tremble. I will do to them according to their way, and according to what they deserve I will judge them; then they shall know that I am the Lord!

Ezekiel 11:10: You shall fall by the sword. I will judge you at the border of Israel. Then you shall know that I am the Lord.

Ezekiel 11:12: And you shall know that I am the Lord; for you have not walked in My statutes nor executed My judgments, but have done according to the customs of the Gentiles which are all around you.

Ezekiel 12:15: Then they shall know that I am the Lord, when I scatter them among the nations and disperse them throughout the countries.

Ezekiel 12:16: But I will spare a few of their men from the sword, from famine, and from pestilence, that they may declare all their abominations among the Gentiles wherever they go. Then they shall know that I am the Lord.

Ezekiel 12:20: Then the cities that are inhabited shall be laid waste, and the land shall become desolate; and you shall know that I am the Lord.

Ezekiel 12:25: "For I am the Lord. I speak, and the word which I speak will come to pass; it will no more be postponed; for in your days, O rebellious house, I will say the word and perform it," says the Lord God.

Ezekiel 13:9: My hand will be against the prophets who envision futility and who divine lies; they shall not be in the assembly of My people, nor be written in the record of the house of Israel, nor shall they enter into the land of Israel. Then you shall know that I am the Lord God.

Ezekiel 13:14: So I will break down the wall you have plastered with untempered mortar, and bring it down to the ground, so that its foundation will be uncovered; it will fall, and you shall be consumed in the midst of it. Then you shall know that I am the Lord.

Ezekiel 13:21: I will also tear off your veils and deliver My people out of your hand, and they shall no longer be as prey in your hand. Then you shall know that I am the Lord.

Ezekiel 13:23: Therefore you shall no longer envision futility nor practice divination; for I will deliver

My people out of your hand, and you shall know that I am the Lord.

Ezekiel 14:8: I will set My face against that man and make him a sign and a proverb, and I will cut him off from the midst of My people. Then you shall know that I am the Lord.

Ezekiel 15:7: And I will set My face against them. They will go out from one fire, but another fire shall devour them. Then you shall know that I am the Lord, when I set My face against them.

Ezekiel 16:62: And I will establish My covenant with you. Then you shall know that I am the Lord.

Ezekiel 17:21: All his fugitives with all his troops shall fall by the sword, and those who remain shall be scattered to every wind; and you shall know that I, the Lord, have spoken.

Ezekiel 17:24: And all the trees of the field shall know that I, the Lord, have brought down the high tree and exalted the low tree, dried up the green tree and made the dry tree flourish; I, the Lord, have spoken and have done it.

Ezekiel 20:5: Say to them, 'Thus says the Lord God: "On the day when I chose Israel and raised My hand in an oath to the descendants of the house of Jacob, and made Myself known to them in the land of Egypt, I raised My hand in an oath to them, saying, 'I am the Lord your God.'"

Ezekiel 20:7: Then I said to them, 'Each of you, throw away the abominations which are before his eyes, and do not defile yourselves with the idols of Egypt. I am the Lord your God.'

Ezekiel 20:12: Moreover I also gave them My Sabbaths, to be a sign between them and Me, that they might know that I am the Lord who sanctifies them.

Ezekiel 20:19: I am the Lord your God: Walk in My statutes, keep My judgments, and do them.

Ezekiel 20:20: Hallow My Sabbaths, and they will be a sign between Me and you, that you may know that I am the Lord your God.

Ezekiel 20:26: And I pronounced them unclean because of their ritual gifts, in that they caused all their firstborn to pass through the fire, that I might make them desolate and that they might know that I am the Lord.

Ezekiel 20:38: I will purge the rebels from among you, and those who transgress against Me; I will bring them out of the country where they dwell, but they shall not enter the land of Israel. Then you will know that I am the Lord.

Ezekiel 20:42: Then you shall know that I am the Lord, when I bring you into the land of Israel, into the country for which I raised My hand in an oath to give to your fathers.

Ezekiel 20:44: "Then you shall know that I am the Lord, when I have dealt with you for My name's sake, not according to your wicked ways nor according to your corrupt doings, O house of Israel," says the Lord God.

Ezekiel 21:5: That all flesh may know that I, the Lord, have drawn My sword out of its sheath; it shall not return anymore.

Ezekiel 22:16: You shall defile yourself in the sight of the nations; then you shall know that I am the Lord.

Ezekiel 22:22: As silver is melted in the midst of a furnace, so shall you be melted in its midst; then you shall know that I, the Lord, have poured out My fury on you.

Ezekiel 23:49: They shall repay you for your lewdness, and you shall pay for your idolatrous sins. Then you shall know that I am the Lord God.

Ezekiel 24:14: "I, the Lord, have spoken it; it shall come to pass, and I will do it; I will not hold back, nor will I spare, nor will I relent; according to your ways and according to your deeds they will judge you," says the Lord God.

Ezekiel 24:24: Thus Ezekiel is a sign to you; according to all that he has done you shall do; and when this comes, you shall know that I am the Lord God.

Ezekiel 24:27: On that day your mouth will be opened to him who has escaped; you shall speak and no longer be mute. Thus you will be a sign to them, and they shall know that I am the Lord.

Ezekiel 25:5: And I will make Rabbah a stable for camels and Ammon a resting place for flocks. Then you shall know that I am the Lord.

Ezekiel 25:7: Indeed, therefore, I will stretch out My hand against you, and give you as plunder to the nations; I will cut you off from the peoples, and I will cause you to perish from the countries; I will destroy you, and you shall know that I am the Lord.

Ezekiel 25:11: And I will execute judgments upon Moab, and they shall know that I am the Lord.

Ezekiel 25:17: I will execute great vengeance on them with furious rebukes; and they shall know that I am the Lord, when I lay My vengeance upon them.

Ezekiel 26:6: Also her daughter villages which are in the fields shall be slain by the sword. Then they shall know that I am the Lord.

Ezekiel 26:14: 'I will make you like the top of a rock; you shall be a place for spreading nets, and you shall never be rebuilt, for I the Lord have spoken,' says the Lord God.

Ezekiel 28:22: And say, 'Thus says the Lord God: "Behold, I am against you, O Sidon; I will be glorified in your midst; and they shall know that I am the Lord, when I execute judgments in her and am hallowed in her."'

Ezekiel 28:23: For I will send pestilence upon her, and blood in her streets; the wounded shall be judged in her midst by the sword against her on every side; then they shall know that I am the Lord.

Ezekiel 28:24: "And there shall no longer be a pricking brier or a painful thorn for the house of Israel from among all who are around them, who despise them. Then they shall know that I am the Lord God."

Ezekiel 28:26: And they will dwell safely there, build houses, and plant vineyards; yes, they will dwell securely, when I execute judgments on all those around them who despise them. Then they shall know that I am the Lord their God.

Ezekiel 29:6: Then all the inhabitants of Egypt shall know that I am the Lord, because they have been a staff of reed to the house of Israel.

Ezekiel 29:9: And the land of Egypt shall become desolate and waste; then they will know that I am the Lord, because he said, 'The River is mine, and I have made it.'

Ezekiel 29:16: No longer shall it be the confidence of the house of Israel, but will remind them of their iniquity when they turned to follow them. Then they shall know that I am the Lord God.

Ezekiel 29:21: In that day I will cause the horn of the house of Israel to spring forth, and I will open your mouth to speak in their midst. Then they shall know that I am the Lord.

Ezekiel 30:8: Then they will know that I am the Lord, when I have set a fire in Egypt and all her helpers are destroyed.

Ezekiel 30:12: I will make the rivers dry, and sell the land into the hand of the wicked; I will make the land waste, and all that is in it, by the hand of aliens. I, the Lord, have spoken.

Ezekiel 30:19: Thus I will execute judgments on Egypt, then they shall know that I am the Lord.

Ezekiel 30:25: Thus I will strengthen the arms of the king of Babylon, but the arms of Pharaoh shall fall down; they shall know that I am the Lord, when I put My sword into the hand of the king of Babylon and he stretches it out against the land of Egypt.

Ezekiel 30:26: I will scatter the Egyptians among the nations and disperse them throughout the countries. Then they shall know that I am the Lord.

Ezekiel 32:15: When I make the land of Egypt desolate, and the country is destitute of all that once filled it, when I strike all who dwell in it, then they shall know that I am the Lord.

Ezekiel 33:29: Then they shall know that I am the Lord, when I have made the land most desolate because of all their abominations which they have committed.

Ezekiel 34:24: And I, the Lord, will be their God, and My servant David a prince among them; I, the Lord, have spoken.

Ezekiel 34:27: Then the trees of the field shall yield their fruit, and the earth shall yield her increase. They shall be safe in their land; and they shall know that I am the Lord, when I have broken the bands of their yoke and delivered them from the hand of those who enslaved them.

Ezekiel 34:30: "Thus they shall know that I, the Lord their God, am with them, and they, the house of Israel, are My people," says the Lord God.

Who Am I?

Ezekiel 35:4: I shall lay your cities waste, and you shall be desolate. Then you shall know that I am the Lord.

Ezekiel 35:9: I will make you perpetually desolate, and your cities shall be uninhabited; then you shall know that I am the Lord.

Ezekiel 35:12: Then you shall know that I am the Lord. I have heard all your blasphemies which you have spoken against the mountains of Israel, saying, 'They are desolate; they are given to us to consume.'

Ezekiel 35:15: As you rejoiced because the inheritance of the house of Israel was desolate, so I will do to you; you shall be desolate, O Mount Seir, as well as all of Edom—all of it! Then they shall know that I am the Lord.

Ezekiel 36:11: I will multiply upon you man and beast; and they shall increase and bear young; I will make you inhabited as in former times, and do better for you than at your beginnings. Then you shall know that I am the Lord.

Ezekiel 36:23: "And I will sanctify My great name, which has been profaned among the nations, which you have profaned in their midst; and the nations shall know that I am the Lord," says the Lord God, "when I am hallowed in you before their eyes."

Ezekiel 36:36: Then the nations which are left all around you shall know that I, the Lord, have rebuilt the ruined places and planted what was desolate. I, the Lord, have spoken it, and I will do it.

Ezekiel 36:38: Like a flock offered as holy sacrifices, like the flock at Jerusalem on its feast days, so shall the ruined cities be filled with flocks of men. Then they shall know that I am the Lord.

Ezekiel 37:6: I will put sinews on you and bring flesh upon you, cover you with skin and put breath in you; and you shall live. Then you shall know that I am the Lord.

Ezekiel 37:13: Then you shall know that I am the Lord, when I have opened your graves, O My people, and brought you up from your graves.

Ezekiel 37:14: "I will put My Spirit in you, and you shall live, and I will place you in your own land. Then you shall know that I, the Lord, have spoken it and performed it," says the Lord.

Ezekiel 37:28: The nations also will know that I, the Lord, sanctify Israel, when My sanctuary is in their midst forevermore.

Ezekiel 38:23: Thus I will magnify Myself and sanctify Myself, and I will be known in the eyes of many nations. Then they shall know that I am the Lord.

Ezekiel 39:6: And I will send fire on Magog and on those who live in security in the coastlands. Then they shall know that I am the Lord.

Ezekiel 39:7: So I will make My holy name known in the midst of My people Israel, and I will not let them profane My holy name anymore. Then the nations shall know that I am the Lord, the Holy One in Israel.

Ezekiel 39:22: So the house of Israel shall know that I am the Lord their God from that day forward.

Ezekiel 39:28: Then they shall know that I am the Lord their God, who sent them into captivity among the nations, but also brought them back to their land, and left none of them captive any longer.

Hosea 12:9: But I am the Lord your God, ever since the land of Egypt; I will again make you dwell in tents, as in the days of the appointed feast.

Hosea 13:4: Yet I am the Lord your God ever since the land of Egypt, and you shall know no God but Me; for there is no savior besides Me.

Joel 2:27: Then you shall know that I am in the midst of Israel: I am the Lord your God and there is no other. My people shall never be put to shame.

Joel 3:17: So you shall know that I am the Lord your God, dwelling in Zion My holy mountain. Then

Jerusalem shall be holy, and no aliens shall ever pass through her again.

Zechariah 10:6: I will strengthen the house of Judah, and I will save the house of Joseph. I will bring them back, because I have mercy on them. They shall be as though I had not cast them aside; for I am the Lord their God, and I will hear them.

HERE IS WHO JESUS SAID HE WAS

You don't ever have to wonder who Jesus is; here He tells you. I went through the trouble of finding the verses for you. You have no excuse as to why you don't know who Jesus is because I have listed every Scripture that tells you His identity. Study to show yourself approved, not man, but you. Jesus is our example of how we are to be with the Father.

Matthew 22:32: 'I am the God of Abraham, the God of Isaac, and the God of Jacob.' God is not the God of the dead, but of the living.

Matthew 24:5: For many will come in My name, saying, 'I am the Christ,' and will deceive many.

Matthew 27:43: He trusted in God; let Him deliver Him now if He will have Him; for He said, 'I am the Son of God.'

Mark 12:26: But concerning the dead, that they rise, have you not read in the book of Moses, in the burning bush passage, how God spoke to him, saying, 'I am the

God of Abraham, the God of Isaac, and the God of Jacob'?

Luke 1:38: Then Mary said, "Behold the maidservant of the Lord! Let it be to me according to your word." And the angel departed from her.

John 1:23: He said: "I am 'The voice of one crying in the wilderness: "Make straight the way of the Lord,"' as the prophet Isaiah said."

John 6:35: And Jesus said to them, "I am the bread of life. He who comes to Me shall never hunger, and he who believes in Me shall never thirst."

John 6:41: The Jews then complained about Him, because He said, "I am the bread which came down from heaven."

John 6:48: I am the bread of life.

John 6:51: I am the living bread which came down from heaven. If anyone eats of this bread, he will live forever; and the bread that I shall give is My flesh, which I shall give for the life of the world.

John 8:12: Then Jesus spoke to them again, saying, "I am the light of the world. He who follows Me shall not walk in darkness, but have the light of life."

John 8:18: I am One who bears witness of Myself, and the Father who sent Me bears witness of Me.

John 9:5: As long as I am in the world, I am the light of the world.

John 9:9: Some said, "This is he." Others said, "He is like him." He said, "I am he."

John 10:7: Then Jesus said to them again, "Most assuredly, I say to you, I am the door of the sheep."

John 10:9: I am the door. If anyone enters by Me, he will be saved, and will go in and out and find pasture.

John 10:11: I am the good shepherd. The good shepherd gives His life for the sheep.

John 10:14: I am the good shepherd; and I know My sheep, and am known by My own.

John 10:36: Do you say of Him whom the Father sanctified and sent into the world, 'You are blaspheming,' because I said, 'I am the Son of God'?

John 11:25: Jesus said to her, "I am the resurrection and the life. He who believes in Me, though he may die, he shall live."

John 14:6: Jesus said to him, "I am the way, the truth, and the life. No one comes to the Father except through Me."

John 15:1: I am the true vine, and My Father is the vinedresser.

John 15:5: I am the vine, you are the branches. He who abides in Me, and I in him, bears much fruit; for without Me you can do nothing.

Act 7:32: Saying, 'I am the God of your fathers—the God of Abraham, the God of Isaac, and the God of Jacob.' And Moses trembled and dared not look.

Revelation 1:17: And when I saw Him, I fell at His feet as dead. But He laid His right hand on me, saying to me, "Do not be afraid; I am the First and the Last."

Revelation 21:6: And He said to me, "It is done! I am the Alpha and the Omega, the Beginning and the End. I will give of the fountain of the water of life freely to him who thirsts."

Revelation 22:13: I am the Alpha and the Omega, the Beginning and the End, the First and the Last.

Revelation 22:16: "I, Jesus, have sent My angel to testify to you these things in the churches. I am the Root and the Offspring of David, the Bright and Morning Star."

Jesus, is the infallible Word of God. He is the living Word and the true Word of the Father. He is the walking, breathing Word of God Almighty. This is what makes Him the only begotten Son of God. God created a body for His Word to live in and that body was Jesus. We don't worship the Word, we worship and praise the

Father. We go through the Word to gain access to the Father. Let us not be ignorant any longer. We are not to praise Jesus, we are to thank Him for giving up His life that we may live in right relationship with the Father. We seek to know the Father, and we do this by looking at how Jesus lived on the earth as a Son. God gave us the right to be sons of His when Jesus died and rose again.

If we truly want to know who we are, we must first know and understand who God is. Jesus shows us the Father's compassion and love as He only does and says what the Father has done and said. Study the life of Jesus, not to worship Him, but to get to know the Father though Him. If you don't know the Father, you will never know who you are.

> *These things I have spoken to you, that you should not be made to stumble. They will put you out of the synagogues; yes, the time is coming that whoever kills you will think that he offers God service. And these things they will do to you because they have not known the Father nor Me. But these things I have told you, that when the time comes, you may remember that I told you of them. And these things I did not say to you at the beginning, because I was with you. I still have many*

> things to say to you, but you cannot bear them now. However, when He, the Spirit of truth, has come, He will guide you into all truth; for He will not speak on His own authority, but whatever He hears He will speak; and He will tell you things to come. He will glorify Me, for He will take of what is Mine and declare it to you. (John 16:1-4,12-14).

This is what Jesus told His disciples before He went to the cross. I am leaving this with you as a reminder that you have a Comforter, Guide and Someone walking with you to lead and guide you. This is the Holy Spirit. Allow the Holy Spirit to come in and shape you into who God designed you to be. Then you will be able to say with full authority: I am who I AM says that I AM.

www.ingramcontent.com/pod-product-compliance
Lightning Source LLC
Chambersburg PA
CBHW072008110526
44592CB00012B/1237